397 Ways
TO SAVE
M🍁NEY

397 Ways TO SAVE M🍁NEY

Spend Smarter & Live Well on Less

KERRY K. TAYLOR
CREATOR OF
SQUAWKFOX.COM

Collins

397 Ways to Save Money
Copyright © 2009 by Kerry K. Taylor

Published by Collins, an imprint of HarperCollins Publishers Ltd.

First published by Collins in an original trade paperback edition: 2009
This paperback edition: 2011

HarperCollins books may be purchased for educational, business, or
sales promotional use through our Special Markets Department.

HarperCollins Publishers Ltd
2 Bloor Street East, 20th Floor
Toronto, Ontario, Canada
M4W 1A8

www.harpercollins.ca

Library and Archives Canada Cataloguing in Publication
information is available

ISBN 978-1-44341-218-6

Printed and bound in the United States
RRD 9 8 7 6 5 4 3 2 1

To Carl Russmann, my partner and support
in all things, including writing.

Contents

INTRODUCTION

Money Matters

Believe it or not, you have money. It's hard to see it, but hidden in among tax bills, mortgage or rent payments, bags of groceries, debt repayments and all the myriad costs of daily life, there's money waiting to be saved—you just need to know where to look.

And that's what this book is for: to take the challenge out of saving money by showing you hundreds of painless ways to spend smarter and save more for yourself without scrimping or pinching pennies. I'll show you how to avoid the traps we all fall for—buying slick brand-name products, watching the bank ding you with fees, shelling out too much for shelter, getting zapped by energy bills and feeling the pinch at the gas pump—and prevent these huge costs from eroding your hard-earned dollars. I'll show you how simple tricks like raising deductibles on your insurance, shopping smartly online, switching banks and buying more foods with less packaging can help your savings add up to thousands annually. You'll see how even the most basic switches, like changing the way you do laundry or how you prepare meals, can save you hundreds without even trying. It might be hard to believe your life could be full living on less. But it can. And I'll show you how.

In my own life I've discovered that saving money is fun and somewhat addictive. I came from a family who valued saving, so when I found myself in a whole mess of student debt after university, I decided I needed to get out of it as quickly as possible. By making simple changes, rethinking which costs mattered in my life and picking up a whole bunch of economical new habits, I not only dug myself out of debt in six months but went on to save my way to a six-figure portfolio—and budget-friendly living just stuck with me. Once my debt was gone and as my earnings increased, my cost-cutting ways meant I was spending less on unimportant things, leaving more for things that mattered to me. I started my blog at squawkfox.com because friends wanted me to show them how I could possibly live on less but have more to show for it, and I discovered along the way how frugal living is not only profitable but a lot of fun. I wrote this book to share these thrifty tips and techniques so you too can find your lost money without sacrificing what is important to you.

The book is divided into three parts. Part 1 covers your biggest expenses—shelter, financial choices and shopping habits—and shows you where your money goes and how to get it back. Part 2 reveals the sneaky expenses you don't see every day and gives you the tools you need to maintain your stuff, power your home and clean for less. Part 3 takes you on a room-by-room tour of your home, giving you the blueprint to savings everywhere you live.

You've waited too long to save your money and keep more from your paycheque. Read on and find 397 ways to save more and live well on less while having fun. You may just laugh yourself all the way to your no-fee bank account.

PART ONE

Big Decisions

The place you live, the ways you bank and the stuff you buy all have a huge impact on how much you have left at the end of the month. It may sound obvious, but finding ways to cut back in areas that have become ingrained habits like housing and banking can be difficult. But it's amazing to see how rethinking these core choices in everyday life and making a few smart money decisions can reap big savings in a short time. Read on to see how you can save thousands of dollars on housing costs and financial fees, and learn numerous shopping tactics to help you save more while spending less.

CHAPTER 1

Renting

Renting can make you rich. That's the kind of statement that runs against almost everything our society tells us about property ownership, but it's true. Under the right circumstances and with the right strategies, renting can be one of the thriftiest decisions you can make—and, because shelter expenses account for so much of our monthly budgets, it can be a big way to save. Most people would be surprised to know I built up a six-figure portfolio *and* paid off $17,000 in student debt while renting a modest basement suite in Vancouver, B.C. I had more than enough money for a down payment on a condo an hour outside of Vancouver, but I made the decision to continue renting to save more money. My reasons for renting were based on hard financial facts rather than emotion.

The cost of real estate where I lived was, and still is, astronomical when compared with the rest of Canada. At the time, a small condo far outside of the city was around $300,000, with condo fees ranging from $300 to $500 per month. With my rent being a mere $600 a month including heat, cable and laundry, the choice was clear: given my location within walking distance from work and my ultra-low rent, I could save thousands a year by not paying mortgage interest, condo fees, property tax and transportation costs. And that's just what I did: I lived in my rented apartment and squirrelled away savings—much more in savings, in fact, than I would have gained in home equity.

Many bankers, real estate agents and mortgage brokers would like you to believe home ownership is the best path to wealth. But renting can have huge advantages for those who pay low rent because they have either made housing sacrifices or live in a rent-controlled building. Renting also offers flexibility to those requiring a place for months or a few years. It's a lot easier and less expensive to give notice on an apartment than it is to sell a house.

If you're looking to rent a house or apartment, the Canada Mortgage and Housing Corporation (CMHC) suggests your monthly shelter costs—including rent, electricity, heat, water and municipal services—should be less than 30% of your before-tax household income. This calculation does not include the costs of renters insurance, parking or amenities like cable, phone and Internet access. So before pounding the pavement looking for the perfect rental, add up your living costs and consider your level of income. It makes no financial sense to rent a place that leaves you with little savings at the end of the month.

If you've made the decision to be a renter rather than a homeowner, there are common ways you can save money on rent.

➤ **Rent less apartment.** Renters have many housing options: high-rise and low-rise apartments, townhouses, condos, detached homes, basement suites and duplexes. As a general rule, units on upper-level floors cost more than units closer to the ground—or under it! So steer clear of penthouses and opt for the ground level in buildings. Downsizing your apartment can also save you hundreds a month, because a smaller space costs less to rent. Renting a smaller space has the added benefits of reducing your energy costs and requiring fewer furnishings.

BOTTOM LINE: A modest rent reduction of even $100 per month saves you $1,200 a year. Multiply this by three years and you've saved $3,600, plus compound interest.

➤ **Get a place with utilities and amenities included.** Basic monthly rent is a given cost, but sometimes you can find a unit with expensive utilities like heat or cable included in the price. Not having to pay a separate heating or cable bill could save you $60 a month (or $720 a year). Renting with perks like parking can also save you big bucks if you live in a major city and need a place to park your car. Rentals with on-site coin-free laundry can save you upwards of $40 a month, and the convenience of not having to search for loonies to get your undies clean is priceless.

BOTTOM LINE: Turn up the heat and park your car for less by renting an apartment with utilities and amenities included in the monthly price—and save $100 per month.

➤ **Check utility costs and connection fees before renting.**
Many renters find the cost of connecting utilities a shock
to their pocketbook when they move into their new place.
Hooking up a phone runs about $35, cable can cost up to
$60, and fees for hydro and Internet add up. Before signing a
rental agreement, find out which utility companies service the
building and contact each company to determine the average
monthly cost. Knowing in advance what your monthly utility bills amount to could save you from renting a place that's
too expensive to heat in the winter. Also, don't be afraid to
ask utility companies to waive connection or transfer fees or
give you a discount—competing businesses like Bell, Shaw
and Rogers all want your monthly business and may cut a
deal to get you onto their service plan. If utility companies are
unable to cite monthly costs, try asking the previous tenants
for average utility prices. Keep in mind, though, that utility
bills can vary drastically depending on individual usage.
**BOTTOM LINE: Doing a little research on monthly utility costs
could save you from renting a place that is too expensive to
heat, while negotiating for lower connection fees could save
you hundreds.**

➤ **Rent closer to work.** Renting closer to your place of
employment can save you from paying for a daily commute or buying a car. Looking for a place within walking
or biking distance is the most frugal scenario, keeps you
fit for free, and will save you time on your commute. Who
doesn't want to spend less time stuck in traffic or waiting
for a bus?

BOTTOM LINE: Paying $100 more a month in rent to live closer to work can save you thousands a year in transportation costs.

➤ **Negotiate monthly rent and yearly increases.** Asking prospective landlords to reduce the rent, even by as little as $20 a month, can add up to hundreds in yearly savings. If there is a high vacancy rate in your area, be sure to negotiate hard in a renter's market because landlords will be competing for your rental dollars. Having a good rental record with excellent references can also bolster your bid for a break on monthly rent. But keep your eye on yearly rent increases as well and negotiate to keep your rent in line at the end of the lease if you want to stay. Being a clean, quiet and prompt-paying tenant may help convince a landlord to freeze rent rather than risk an empty unit or an unknown new tenant. **BOTTOM LINE: Don't let increasing rents deter you from asking for a discount—even $15 a month adds up to an extra $180 in your pocket at the end of the year (enough to cover more than a week's worth of groceries).**

➤ **Get a written tenancy agreement.** Always get the rental rules in writing before moving in. Understand how long you are required to stay, how much notice is required to end the tenancy, the landlord's obligations to maintain the property, and the deposit costs. Knowing the rules in advance can protect you from disagreements and unexpected rent increases. Landlord and tenancy laws vary from province to province, so get familiar with the tenancy act that will apply to you. In some provinces, you'll be entitled to any interest earned on your security deposit—check your local regulations and then make sure your landlord pays up!

BOTTOM LINE: Being familiar with your legal rights today may save you big dollars (and frustration) in the future.

➤ **Get a roommate.** Got an extra bedroom in your apartment? Reduce your rental costs by about 50% by renting or subletting the spare room in your apartment. Use the roommate-finding sections on websites like kijiji.ca and craigslist.ca to post your classified ads for free. Before accepting a roommate, check to make sure your lifestyles are compatible and that you both can deal with the other's schedule. Setting up a written agreement with roommates is also a good idea. If you live close to a college or university, consider renting a room to a student or a young professional. Students tend to spend lots of time in class, making them an ideal absentee roomie. Sharing space saves on utility costs too, since bills can be split.

BOTTOM LINE: Renting out a spare room could save you 50% on your rental and utility costs: splitting the cost of a $1,350 a month rental saves you a whopping $8,100 a year.

➤ **Invest in renters insurance.** Becoming a victim of theft or losing your valuables to water damage can set you back thousands of dollars in property loss. Spend your dollars wisely by investing in renter's insurance. A renter's policy can cover personal property as well as personal liability (in case you are sued for property damage or bodily injury).

Before you call for a quote, calculate how much property protection you require. Do you have $25,000, $40,000 or $100,000 worth of valuables? Do you require additional insurance for camera equipment, a bike or jewellery? Take an inventory of your possessions, listing each item, when you acquired it and the purchase price or current value. Don't just think big-ticket items! In the case of a fire you'd need to replace *everything,* from socks to computers. Totalling up the value of these items will give you a rough idea of what your property is worth—and you may be surprised. Keeping receipts and photos of your property off-site in a safety deposit box can help you if you need to make a claim. You can store records for free by emailing photos and scans to a webmail account. Also, ask your landlord for details about the rental property, including roof condition, type of heating, and the frame construction of the building. Insurance companies want to know the details of your building and the risks to them before offering insurance. Insurance discounts can be found through employer programs or your post-secondary alumni association (if you're a graduate). Other lower-cost policies are available through RBC Insurance and TD Insurance. Asking for a quote is free, and coverage often begins within 24 hours.

BOTTOM LINE: Protect yourself against property loss by getting renter's insurance. A $20 a month policy could save you upwards of $20,000.

➤ **Keep your rental clean.** Living like a slob or causing damage to your landlord's property will cost you your rental deposit. Keeping your place clean and caring for appliances like stoves and refrigerators will help you recover the maximum when you move. Read the fine print in your lease about painting, changing pictures, cleaning carpets and dry cleaning drapes—you may be required to return the space to its original state, which doubles the cost of painting if you decided to paint a formerly beige place bright purple.

BOTTOM LINE: Take care of your apartment according to your lease agreement to recoup your full damage deposit and save hundreds from restoring the place back to perfection.

➤ **Know when it's time to buy.** While buying a home may sound contrary to the advice given at the beginning of this chapter, you may be in the perfect situation to seize a nice piece of real estate given the size of your down payment, the location of the home and whether the housing market favours buyers. When these factors line up, you can gain financially from buying a home instead of renting. For example, assume you are currently paying $1,500 each month in rent but have $30,000 available as a down payment on a home. If you invest this at 5% per year, your $30,000 will grow to almost $105,000 after 25 years. If, on the other hand, you use the $30,000 as a down payment on a $300,000 home at 4.5% over 25 years, your mortgage payments will be $1,578 each month, about the same as your rent. Assuming the property appreciates in value at 2.2% yearly, it will be worth almost $520,000 when paid off. While you won't be able to take advantage of this equity without selling your home (possibly by downsizing), your net worth will be significantly more in this case if you own rather than rent. Remember to budget for the additional costs of maintenance, property taxes and utilities when you're deciding how much you can afford.

BOTTOM LINE: Do the math to see if, with house prices, rental costs and the size of your down payment, buying makes more financial sense than renting. Check out the website for Industry Canada (ic.gc.ca) and use their Rent or Buy Calculator (you'll find a link to it in the A–Z index) to see if you're in a financial position to buy.

CHAPTER 2

Homeownership

Money is a housekeeping item. Without it, you can't keep your house. This was my parents' motto when I was growing up. Our house wasn't large and lavish with a gourmet kitchen or spa bathroom. Our neighbours didn't walk by our home wanting to live like us—but they should have. While they paid for swimming pools and sun rooms, my parents paid off their mortgage and put their savings to work by funding their retirement accounts and helping my sister and me go to university.

There's no doubt that buying and maintaining a home is expensive. There's saving for the down payment, financing the mortgage and replacing the roof when you least expect it. Along with these expenses, there are also variable costs like utilities to consider. Add it all up and you're paying big bucks for home sweet home. Despite the costs, though, buying and owning your own home can be a wise financial decision in the long run. By removing emotion and crunching the numbers, it's clear to see that having a large enough down payment on a property well within your budget and a mortgage with prepayment options can make owning a home financially beneficial.

So before hiring a realtor to go house shopping, it's important to determine how much home you can truly afford. When it comes to determining home affordability, the Canada Mortgage and Housing Corporation (CMHC) recommends that your monthly housing costs should not exceed 32% of your gross household monthly income. If you're carrying other types of debt—car payments, credit card debt, etc.—then your entire monthly debt load should not be more than 40% of your gross monthly income. Don't forget to factor in retirement contributions and other areas requiring your financial attention—such as debt repayment, emergency funds, education for the kids and home maintenance costs. The CMHC's home affordability numbers don't account for your retirement or savings goals, and you may feel stretched if you buy too much house and have little room left for buying furniture or putting away savings.

If you're ready to take the financial leap and land yourself some real estate, there are numerous ways to save money on buying a home and reducing the interest on your mortgage.

➤ **Know what you can afford.** For most of us, our mortgage represents our biggest debt and the only kind financial experts consider "good" debt. But an over-your-head mortgage is one of the quickest routes to bankruptcy. Knowing what you can afford could spare you financial catastrophe in the future. The CMHC website contains questionnaires and calculators for those looking to crunch numbers, and they're well worth your time. An excellent way to see how a mortgage feels is to practice paying it before you buy. Pay your landlord your rent, then take the difference between that amount and your anticipated mortgage cost and put this additional money into a high-interest savings account to use later for your down payment. If you can't come up with this additional monthly cash, then you know the mortgage is too steep and you need to either continue saving for a bigger down payment or look at lower-priced homes.

BOTTOM LINE: It pays to crunch the numbers and know what you can afford before viewing homes and falling in love with a property. A too-high mortgage can leave you resorting to credit cards and lines of credit to pay everyday expenses—a downward spiral that could cost you thousands in interest.

➤ **Get a home inspection before purchasing.** Getting a home inspection done before you make an offer on a home may be the best money you ever spend. A home inspection uncovers unseen problems that may cost you thousands of dollars down the road. A home inspection also serves as a negotiation tool with sellers, as they may fix flagged issues or reduce their selling price. Take the time to find the right home inspector, and be aware that it might not be the one your real estate agent recommends. Check references, ideally from homeowners who have been in their home for a few years so that any potential troubles have surfaced. The CMHC website offers assistance in finding a home inspector near you, or check out *The Holmes Inspection* by Mike Holmes to learn how to get the most out of your inspection.

BOTTOM LINE: Hiring a home inspector before purchasing a home may cost you around $500 but is well worth it considering the thousands you might have to spend to fix unseen problems behind the walls.

➤ **Don't buy someone else's renovation—be cautious of "flipped" homes.** Falling in love with the seemingly fresh look of paint, new flooring or neatly potted plants in the yard can be a financial disaster if the structure of the home is not sound. The finish of the home is important, but be sure to look past a new bathroom or kitchen renovation and learn what lurks beneath the surface. You may discover that new plaster and paint are a facade disguising mould, water damage or a cracked foundation.

BOTTOM LINE: Look past the surface when you're house-hunting, and be cautious about recent renovations. The homeowner may be trying to disguise something that really needs an expensive repair.

➤ **Downsize or buy a smaller home.** Palatial houses cost big bucks in buyers' fees, down payment size, mortgage interest, home maintenance and utilities. Buying a smaller home reduces these costs. Let's assume you pass on a $350,000 home in favour of a less expensive $325,000 property. The price difference of $25,000 is substantial and saves you $5,000 on a 20% down payment. Assuming a 25-year mortgage at a 5.5% interest rate, your monthly payment is $122.81 less, saving you a total of $16,845.25 in interest over 25 years. Add it all up, and a $25,000-less-expensive home saves you $41,845.25 in interest plus principal on the mortgage. (This calculation does not include closing fees and maintenance costs.) The true benefit? Perhaps retire from work a few years sooner. Besides, heating a castle in the middle of a Canadian winter is costly.

BOTTOM LINE: Opting for a smaller home over a larger, more expensive one could save you not only tens of thousands off the sticker price but also thousands more in mortgage interest.

➤ **Make a larger down payment and pay less mortgage loan insurance.** Rushing in to buy a home without a good down payment will cost you in paying higher mortgage loan insurance. The cost for this legally required insurance is a premium of between 0.5% and 2.9% of the total mortgage. If you have a bigger down payment, you pay less mortgage insurance because the loan is no longer classified as a high-ratio mortgage. For example, on a $300,000 home, increasing your down payment from 5% with a premium of 2.75% to a down payment of 20% with a premium of 1% saves you $5,437.50 over 25 years.

BOTTOM LINE: Paying 20% down on a home purchase saves you from paying mortgage loan insurance—money you could use to increase your mortgage payments and pay off your debt faster.

➤ **Don't get sold mortgage life insurance—buy term life insurance.** Mortgage life insurance is a waste of good money. You may need life insurance to provide for your dependants and help meet large financial obligations such as mortgage payments or education for your kids or to put food on the table. But mortgage life insurance is over-priced for the policyholder and lucrative for the policy seller. Generally, mortgage life insurance covers only the outstanding principal on a mortgage should the home-owner pass away. The premiums stay the same even as the mortgage reduces as you pay it off—you pay the same premium for less and less value.

BOTTOM LINE: Put your dollars toward term life insurance to cover your family above and beyond mortgage expenses for half the cost of mortgage life insurance.

➤ **Negotiate your mortgage.** Before sitting down with a prospective mortgage lender, get your credit score to know where you stand. Check out Equifax (equifax.ca) or Trans-Union (transunion.ca) to get your credit score online for about $25. Once you know your credit score, don't be afraid to ask lenders for a better rate. Shop around and play multiple offers off each other. A half a percent rate reduction will save you thousands over the span of your mortgage, so it's well worth your time. If a lender offers you perks like gift certificates for furniture, loyalty card points or a trip, take a pass. These so-called perks come at the cost of a higher rate. If the banks are not budging on their offer, consult with a mortgage broker. Mortgage brokers are paid finder's fees by banks—these fees gener-ally do not differ from bank to bank, so the broker has limited incentive to act outside your best interest, thus finding you the best deal possible.

BOTTOM LINE: Do some research and know your credit score before approaching a lender for a mortgage. Knowing how lenders see you financially can help you to negotiate for better mortgage rates and terms. On a $285,000 mortgage over 25 years, negotiating your rate from 5.5% down to 5% will save you $25,220.32 in interest—so get negotiating.

➤ **Get a mortgage with good prepayment privileges.** A favourably low interest rate is only one criterion when shopping for a mortgage. Look beyond interest rates and ask for a mortgage with prepayment privileges. Prepayments are lump-sum payments you make outside of your normal mortgage payment schedule, where 100% of the payment goes against the principal. Prepayment privileges are your best financial friend because you will pay off your mortgage sooner and save significantly on interest. Also, look for a mortgage that allows you to increase the size of your payment without penalty—so you can take advantage of a raise or extra job.

BOTTOM LINE: Getting a mortgage with prepayment privileges can save you thousands in interest by paying down the principal faster. On a $250,000 mortgage at 6% over 25 years, one prepayment of $1,000 each year will save you $26,671.63 in interest and help you pay off your mortgage two and a half years sooner.

➤ **Pay your mortgage biweekly rather than monthly.** Paying your mortgage every two weeks saves you an astounding amount of money and pays off your mortgage sooner.

With biweekly payments, there will be a few months where three mortgage payments are due, depending on how the weeks fall, but if you are on biweekly paycheques, you won't notice the difference.

BOTTOM LINE: When compared with monthly payments, a biweekly-payment structure saves you $11,000 in interest and ends your mortgage three and a half years sooner. (This calculation assumes a $90,000 loan at 5% interest with a 25-year term.)

➤ **Save big on smart homeowner insurance.** Homeowner insurance deductibles can start at $250. By increasing your deductible to $500, you could save 15% on your insurance costs. The higher your deductible, the bigger your savings, because you're not making multiple smaller claims that would increase your premiums. You could also get up to a 5% discount by installing smoke detectors, carbon monoxide detectors, deadbolt locks and alarms to increase your home security. Another home insurance discount can be had by putting expensive jewellery in a safety deposit box. Most banks charge around $45 a year for a smaller safety deposit box, while larger ones can cost up to $200. Be sure to keep your bank receipt and claim the cost of your safety deposit box on your taxes—it counts as a tax credit!

BOTTOM LINE: Increase deductibles, install smoke detectors and put Grandma's ring in a safety deposit box to reduce the cost of your homeowner insurance and save hundreds of additional dollars per year.

➤ **Move to your basement apartment.** If you're living in a house that's much larger than you need, why not move to your basement apartment for a few years and rent out the upstairs. You could make a huge dent on paying down the principal by keeping your own mortgage contributions steady and adding in the rent. For example, on a $285,000 mortgage at 5.5% over 25 years, your payments are about $1,750 a month. Add the $1,000 you get for renting out the upstairs for 25 years, and you could save $135,555.71 in interest charges and pay off your mortgage 13 years sooner. **BOTTOM LINE: Moving into your basement apartment and renting out the upstairs could help you pay off your mortgage faster, saving you tens of thousands.**

➤ **Buy for the long term.** If you plan on moving in a few years, consider renting instead. Buying a property for the short term rarely makes financial sense. After paying realtor commissions, lawyers' bills, closing costs, land transfer taxes and insurance premiums, the transaction costs on selling real estate are high. To recoup this cash, you'll need to sell your property for roughly 10% more than what you paid for it. In Canada, realtor fees are typically 3% to 7%, paid by the person selling the home. Add moving costs, light renovations and the previously mentioned costs and you're at a financial loss on sale. Stay renting and keep your cash invested in a high-interest savings account. You'll earn a guaranteed return on your investment with a savings account, and have a better down payment when you're ready to stay put for the longer term.

BOTTOM LINE: If you're looking to move in the short term, consider staying in a rental to prevent the costs of selling from eating away at your investment.

CHAPTER 3

Financial Choices

Money can be expensive when you have to spend a lot just for the privilege of saving it. When you look at your annual credit card fees, consider the small, seemingly insignificant charges in your daily bank account and calculate management fees on your portfolio of mutual funds, it all adds up to hundreds and thousands a year! On the whole, Canadians spend far too much money on their finances. But how much is too much? My general rule is if you could be paying less, then you're paying too much.

The surprising part is that reducing both the large and small fees you pay is easy. You don't need to be a certified financial planner or have a PhD in economics to stop the fees from feeding on your cash. A few phone calls and a bit of paperwork will save you hundreds a year.

I must confess that realizing how much my banking and my financial planner were costing me was not a joyous moment. But it wasn't long before I had moved my banking, switched my credit card, transitioned my retirement savings and cut my life insurance premiums in half. Some of these changes took a few hours while others took days. But considering the thousands of dollars I've saved by putting in the effort to manage my money, it certainly added up to a very nice return on my time.

Considering there are quite literally thousands of different ways to manage your money, your financial situation might be similar to mine or it might be vastly different. Regardless of where you're at, there are many opportunities for you to save money on your financial expenses.

Credit Cards

A credit card can be an expensive piece of plastic to carry. With some credit card interest rates over 18%, it's easy to lose a bundle by not paying off monthly balances. If you love paying with plastic, then consider some of these tips to keep hefty interest charges from eating away at your principal dollars.

> ➤ **Switch to a no-fee credit card.** Many gold and platinum credit cards charge a sizable annual fee billed directly to your statement. If you don't regularly use the perks associated with these expensive cards, then switch to a no-fee alternative and still benefit from reward programs. Years ago I paid a $120 annual fee to use a Gold travel credit card. While the romantic notion of travelling the world on reward points was appealing, the reality was I never charged enough to get off the ground. After doing the math, I realized I needed to use the card for four years

and pay $480 in annual fees before collecting enough points to travel to the exotic location of Toronto. At this point I knew this Gold card travel program would never fly for me. When I shopped around and compared the benefits of no-fee cards, I found my wings with the President's Choice Financial MasterCard. This deliciously feeless card offers free groceries for lightweight spenders like myself. By switching credit cards, not only did I save the $120 a year on fees but over the year I collected enough points to cover hundreds in free groceries. There are lots of great options out there—go to the website for the Financial Consumer Agency of Canada (fcac-acfc.gc.ca) to compare credit cards and find the one that works best for you.

BOTTOM LINE: By switching to a no-fee credit card with attainable rewards, I put food on the table for free and saved on annual fees.

➤ **Pay more than the minimum balance.** Paying the bare minimum on your monthly balance only prolongs the debt agony and increases the amount of interest you pay to the credit card company. Save yourself at least 18% in interest charges by paying off your credit card debt every month. Depending on the size of your debt, you may add thousands to your wallet each year. For example, on a starting balance of $1,500 with an annual interest rate of 19%, your debt would be paid off in 8 years and 9 months if you paid only the minimum balance of 4% of the initial balance, or $60 per month. The total interest paid is a staggering $889.77—on an initial loan of only $1,500. If you can't pay your card off in full each month, try to at least double the minimum payment so that you're actually taking a bite out of the principal.

BOTTOM LINE: Pay off your credit cards sooner by putting down more than the minimum and save yourself hundreds— and even thousands—in debt repayment interest.

➤ **Negotiate a lower interest rate.** If you're carrying a balance on your credit card, don't be afraid to call up your issuer and ask for a lower rate. Many lenders will cut you a break if you've been paying the minimum each month, so ask if they will reduce your monthly interest rate.

BOTTOM LINE: It costs you nothing to pick up the phone and negotiate a lower interest rate with your lender and could help you pay off your credit card sooner. A cut in rate from 19.5% to 15% on a $5,000 balance would save you around $225 a year.

➤ **Schedule a card-free day, week or month.** If you love paying in plastic and just can't resist the store displays, then try scheduling card-free days each month. You could save mega moolah by leaving your credit card at home in the freezer or hidden away in a shoebox. An alternative to leaving your card at home is to put a sticky note on the card with a reminder not to spend.

BOTTOM LINE: Look for ways to get by without a credit card for a few days each month to cut back on spending and save you some extra dollars.

How I Paid Off My Student Debt in Six Months

It's been nearly 10 years since I retired my student debt. I'll never forget the mixed feeling when I graduated from school with my bachelor's degree: starting a new life, yet at the same time facing $17,000 of debt. Looking back on those early days makes my stomach lurch and my head ache.

The challenge of repaying student loans is common across Canada. In 2004, Statistics Canada reported that the average student with a bachelor's degree graduated with a $19,500 debt. In comparison, my $17,000 loan doesn't seem as bad, but even back then I knew debt felt bad. I wanted to get the debt monkey off my back, so I made the commitment to myself and to my financial future to get out of student debt fast. Some of my strategies were specific to my age and stage in life, but many of them can be great tactics for anyone looking to crawl out of a big hole of debt. This is how I paid off my $17,000 student loan in just six months.

I negotiated my first job offer. The most important action I took in paying down my student debt was to not jump at my first job offer. So many new graduates get excited about that first offer and accept it quickly, fearing that it's the best they will get. Not true, I say. When you get your first offer, congratulate yourself for starters, and then negotiate for a little bit more. When I got my first offer, I thanked the company wholeheartedly for their offer and stated my excitement about the position and working with their team. I also mentioned how I felt the job was a good fit for my skills and my direction. I kept the happy feeling going by saying I was flexible with compensation. However, would the company consider paying me $X more, as my skills were solid in areas A, B and C? Yes! Surprisingly, this strategy has always worked for me. While my fellow graduates accepted their first offer, I negotiated a better salary—and gave myself more money every two weeks to get rid of that debt.

I kept living like a student and didn't buy stuff. When I graduated from school, I kept my same inexpensive apartment, my same bus pass and my same frugal habits. By continuing to live as I did when I had no money, I didn't increase my cost of living and consume all my newly earned income. I've seen many new graduates land their first job and then go and blow their paycheque on stuff. They might buy a new car or new stereo equipment or rent a bigger apartment. I've even seen new grads buy a condo. But after I graduated I bought only what I needed for work, which was clothing. Essentially, I lived on only one-third of my new salary as a technical writer, and devoted the other two-thirds to killing debt. Instead of keeping up with the Joneses, I kept up with my loan interest and paid down lots of loan principal sooner. Paying down principal quickly prevented my loan from increasing in size with interest charges, saving me thousands over the longer term.

I made a plan. After graduation I had two student loans to pay back, and one had a much higher interest rate than the other. The task was daunting, but I sat down and calculated my monthly after-tax income, my rent and my other living expenses and made a monthly repayment schedule to attack the higher-interest debt first while still paying more than the minimum balance on the second loan. The plan worked. After consistently hitting the principal, I paid off the steeper loan and then reallocated my repayments to the second loan. Making a plan and sticking to it made the huge task of paying back $17,000 manageable on my salary with my living expenses.

I used all available tax credits. In Canada students get tax credits for tuition fees, textbooks and an "education amount" above tuition and textbooks. Every year when tax season rolled around I would fill out my tax return and use many of these available credits to reduce the taxes I paid on income, thus decreasing the loan required for my education. As a student, keeping track of these available tax credits and not losing tax certificates and forms saved me thousands. I saved even more by taking my unclaimed educational credits and carrying them forward to use against my income when I started working.

I saved for retirement. When I started my first job, many in my graduating class thought I was silly for saving for retirement so soon. My friends would say, "I'm only 23 years old, why do I need to start saving now?" The answer is simple: more tax breaks. When you begin your new job and start pulling in a nice salary (because you negotiated better compensation), you pay income tax. Welcome to being an adult. But, if you start contributing to a Registered Retirement Savings Plan (RRSP), you get tax breaks. Along with paying less tax, contributing to an RRSP has the added bonus of giving you the feeling of growing a nest egg. Let's face it, working hard and having nothing to show for it but debt repayment isn't exactly fun. So growing some savings can really make you feel good. When I contributed to my RRSP way back then, I took my tax refund and used it to pay down more student loan debt. Consider this tax break the new math: you contribute to retirement, you get tax breaks, you get tax refunds, you feed the refund to your debt. This is how you win the "get out of student debt fast" game. ■

➤ **Read the fine print:** Credit cards may seem like a shopping gift from heaven, but remember they're financial instruments designed to make banks money. So read the fine print before you sign up for anything, and play by the rules. Some cards may offer enticing introductory rates on balance transfers but will escalate those rates instantly if you miss even one payment. Other cards will apply the lower rate only to your balance transfer and then charge you a higher rate on purchases—but will apply your payments only to the balance transfer until it's paid off, so you're racking up interest on anything you add to the card.

BOTTOM LINE: Understanding what's on offer with your credit card helps you to maximize your savings and minimize any nasty shocks when your bill arrives. If you add $1,000 in purchases to a balance of $5,000 on a credit card that gives you only 6.3% on the balance transfer, you could pile up around $700 worth of debt in interest charges in the three years that $1,000 compounds at 18% before you pay it off.

Banking

I've been known to fire a few big banks in my lifetime because of their high service fees on chequing accounts and low interest rates for savings. I'm always polite when I hand a banker a pink slip, but I'm more than happy to move my money to banks that give customers competitive rates.

Don't stick around in a relationship just because it's a pain to move your money to a new bank. Take a good hard look at how many service fee dings you've paid and consider switching banks to get the best bank for your buck. Here are some tips for finding the best deal in banking.

> ➤ **Banish banking fees.** I dare you to add up all your banking fees. Go ahead, open your statements and calculate your monthly account fees, minimum balance fees, withdrawal fees, cheque-cashing fees, moving-money fees, paying-bills fees and ATM fees, fees and more fees. Depending on your banking habits, all these tiny transaction fees and charges can add up to hundreds a year just for accessing your money. If you're done with getting dinged, then consider visiting the Financial Consumer Agency of Canada online (fcac-acfc.gc.ca) to compare which banks offer the best deals for your specific banking needs. After visiting this site myself several years ago, I made the decision to fire my current fee-happy bank and open accounts with online banks ING Direct and President's Choice Financial. By making the switch,

I stopped paying banking fees altogether and have saved hundreds over the years.

BOTTOM LINE: Banking fees can be a lucrative business for big Canadian banks and can eat away at your savings over time. Consider switching to a no-fee chequing account to minimize your banking fees and to access your money without being charged. Even if you only save the account charge of $15 per month, that still adds up to $180 a year saved for the exact same service.

➤ **Negotiate lower banking fees.** Walking into your bank and asking for a better deal on fees is free. If you're a good customer and ask nicely, many banks are open to waiving fees and service charges to keep you banking. Many times a banking representative will review your banking habits and find a better plan within that financial institution, saving you big dollars each month.

BOTTOM LINE: Comparing the different accounts within your financial institution and negotiating for lower banking fees can be time well spent and save you dozens of dollars each year.

➤ **Change your ATM habits.** Planning your cash withdrawals ahead of time can save you lots of money in ATM charges over the span of a year. Axe your ATM fees by using only your bank's machines, withdrawing cash only a few times a month and knowing how many free ATM visits per month you're allowed for your particular account. If your account's ATM fees don't jive with your banking needs, consider switching plans within your financial institution to get a better deal.

BOTTOM LINE: Saving four $1.50 ATM charges each month adds up to $72 a year in savings.

➤ **Open a high-interest savings account.** If you're keeping a few bucks sitting around in your chequing account, then move your savings to a high-interest account, like those offered through online banks ING Direct or President's Choice Financial or credit unions Achieva Financial or Outlook Financial. (Many of the big banks also offer high-interest accounts, but watch out for restrictions and fees.)

BOTTOM LINE: Open a high-interest savings account and make about 3% more on your savings each year, rather than almost nothing offered through standard bank accounts. On a $1,000 deposit this adds around $30 to your savings in the first year and more in subsequent years with compound interest.

Investing and Insurance

When it comes to saving lots of loonies, it helps to think in terms of both long- and short-term needs. Investment vehicles like retirement savings plans and tax-free savings accounts fit the bill to store your cash and keep you safe for retirement, and emergency funds, wills and insurance all guarantee that your frugal habits will serve you and your family in times of need. Here are some simple suggestions for saving on your long-term financial choices.

➤ **Pay off your debt.** The single best financial investment you can make is to pay off your debt. Whether you have a car loan, mortgage, student loans, line of credit or credit card balance, reducing your debt saves you thousands and just makes you feel good. Every dollar you put down on debt gives you an immediate tax-free return on the interest you otherwise would have paid.

BOTTOM LINE: Before investing in the latest stock market darling, pay down your debt and reduce the interest paid to creditors to save thousands. For example, putting $5,000 against a debt at 12% saves you around $634 of interest in one year. That's a pretty good rate of return for a $5,000 investment.

➤ **Lower your investment fees.** I learned about investment fees three years after opening my first Registered Retirement Savings Plan (RRSP). I was excited to be saving for my retirement early on and looked forward to the income tax breaks for contributing a fair chunk of my salary. Back then I happily handed my money over to a financial adviser who invested my retirement contributions in mutual funds. But after watching my portfolio consistently (and significantly) lag the financial indexes, I took a closer look at my investments. I quickly discovered the impact that fees called management expense ratios (MERs) and loads could have on my retirement savings. Doing the math, my MER of 3.25% on a $25,000 portfolio was costing me around $813 a year and totalled $2,438 over three years, not including the loss of compound interest. Being a younger investor with zero desire to pay hundreds of thousands of dollars in fees by the time I turned 65, I decided to find a less expensive way to invest for my future. The answer came by accident when my neighbour's copy of *MoneySense* magazine landed in my mailbox. The cover story touted low-cost index funds and an investment strategy with the silly name of "The Couch Potato Portfolio." After researching index funds and learning how they passively track market indexes with ultra-low fees, I filled out the forms and moved my entire RRSP to a discount brokerage where I embarked upon becoming a do-it-yourself-investor. Years later I still invest in a diversified portfolio of index funds and shudder to think how much I might otherwise have spent in investment fees. To learn more about how to invest in low-cost index funds, visit moneysense.ca and check out the Couch Potato Portfolio.

BOTTOM LINE: By moving my RRSP from high-fee mutual funds with a 3.25% MER to a balanced portfolio of index funds with a 0.40% MER, I saved myself $713 on investment costs in the first year alone, since the Couch Potato Portfolio fees totalled only $100 a year.

➤ **Open a Tax-Free Savings Account (TFSA).** If you're 18 or older, go to your favourite financial institution and open a TFSA to save $5,000 in cash, stocks or bonds every year tax free. The TFSA is a brilliant vehicle for Canadians looking to stash some extra after-tax cash for a rainy day or to save for a new home, car or even for retirement. Over time the savings with a TFSA can really add up. For example, let's assume you have $25,000 invested in a standard high-interest savings account at 3%. After one year you will earn $760.40 compounded monthly. Depending on your income tax bracket, the government takes around $225. With a TFSA, you get to keep everything. The TFSA is also far more flexible than an RRSP: you can withdraw without any penalties, and the contribution room is always available. Take a look at the Government of Canada's TFSA website (tfsa.gc.ca) for more information.

BOTTOM LINE: Putting money into a TFSA saves you from paying taxes on income earned in the account. For example, investing $5,000 at 4.5% gives you $225 tax free.

➤ **Contribute to your Registered Retirement Savings Plan (RRSP).** Save thousands a year by contributing up to 18% of your pre-tax income to an RRSP. Saving for retirement is a good idea, and contributing to an RRSP is a wonderful way of lowering your taxable income. You can also use your RRSP as an interest-free loan for education or an interest-free down payment toward your first home. Check out the homepage of the Canada Revenue Agency (cra-arc.gc.ca) to find out more about RRSPs.

BOTTOM LINE: Starting an RRSP and contributing up to 18% of your pre-tax income per year lowers your taxable income and saves you hundreds and thousands. For example, a person earning $50,000 a year can contribute up to $9,000 to an RRSP and get a tax refund of about $2,925.

Save for Your Child's Education

Saving for your child's university education can be scarier than retirement planning, because high-school graduation is probably approaching more quickly than your golden years. Don't be taken in by investment firms that tell you that you need to save $100,000 per child: they usually overstate the costs of education to attract more of your money. If you can save even a third of that, you're doing much better than most. Here's how to get started:

- The earlier you start to save, the more time your investments have to grow, so open a Registered Education Savings Plan (RESP) as soon as possible after your child is born. The first step is to get a social insurance number for your child. You'll find the application at servicecanada.gc.ca.

- Choose an RESP with the lowest possible fees. This usually means avoiding those well-advertised "scholarship trusts," where you purchase units in a pooled investment. It makes more sense to use the discount brokerage affiliated with the bank where you do your daily banking.

- Any fees you pay to an investment adviser or mutual fund manager will eat up your returns. The best low-cost investment strategy is to buy index mutual funds or exchange-traded funds (ETFs) through your discount brokerage. For more information, search the web for "index investing."

- Take full advantage of the Canada Education Savings Grant. The federal government will top up every RESP contribution by 20% to 40%, depending on your income, to a maximum of $500 annually and $7,200 over the lifetime of the plan. If you collect the maximum grant amount, it can add up to a free year of university for your child.

- See whether you are eligible for other education grants. The Canada Learning Bond is a one-time grant of $500, plus annual payments of $100 (maximum $2,000), made to low-income parents who open an RESP. The Alberta Centennial Education Savings Plan is similar, and it's available to all Albertans with a child born in 2005 or later, regardless of income. ■

➤ **Invest monthly in your RRSP.** Investing in an RRSP is a smart choice no matter when you do it, but investing monthly (or even bi-weekly) is even smarter. Making monthly payments gives you a few different advantages. For starters, it gets your money into the investment cycle earlier—allowing it more time to grow. It also makes sure that your best RRSP intentions don't get washed aside in a February cash crunch by splitting your contributions evenly over the year at a planned rate. Finally, you can take advantage of dollar cost averaging—an investment strategy that argues market risk can be mitigated by making frequent set investments rather than trying to time lump sum contributions. Essentially, with dollar cost averaging you get exposure to the market both when it is low (which means you get more shares) and when it is high (which means you get fewer shares), and therefore can end up lowering your average price. This can leave you better off than being forced to buy at a particular rate at the end of February. To maximize this strategy, though, make sure your RRSP investment has low or no transaction fees so that you're not getting dinged at each contribution.

BOTTOM LINE: Buy early and buy often when it comes to your RRSP contributions, so that you can watch your diversified investment add up. For example, if you put $5,000 into your RRSP in monthly installments of $416.66 throughout the year instead of in one lump sum at the end of the year, at a 5% return you can gain an extra $116.10 of tax-free growth.

➤ **Don't insure your kids.** The general purpose of life insurance is to serve as income replacement for the insured's dependants. Because children are dependants, rather than having dependants, it makes little financial sense to insure your kids. Many parents buy insurance policies for their children because an agent sells them on the investment aspect of a cash value policy. Pass on these expensive policies, which are lucrative for the selling agent, and open a real investment that your kids can benefit from, like a Registered Education Savings Plan (RESP) for your child's post-secondary education. Unlike a cash value life insurance policy for children, an RESP has real advantages where the earnings are sheltered from tax until drawn out for the child's education, and then taxed at the child's marginal rate.

BOTTOM LINE: Don't get sold on buying life insurance for your kids. Opt instead to buy life insurance for the breadwinners in your family. To invest in your children's future, consider opening an RESP to help fund their post-secondary education.

➤ **Make a will.** A will won't specifically save you any money, but it can save your estate from probate fees, determine distribution of your estate and can help prevent disputes among heirs. For those who want to leave everything to one person, a do-it-yourself will kit for around $50 might be enough but could leave much open for will challenges. A better route to take, especially if you have children, is to spend the $500 and hire a lawyer. Unlike a will kit, lawyers can answer specific questions and deal with your individual situation.

BOTTOM LINE: Hire a lawyer and spend the $500 on a will to protect your assets for your children and heirs.

➤ **Get term life insurance not cash value insurance.** If you have a family to support, then get term life insurance. Term life is pure life insurance in that you pay an annual premium to receive a decided amount of coverage. When the policyholder dies, the beneficiaries collect, and there is no other potential payout to the policy. All other policies have an additional investment angle to them, and so are sold as having added "value." They can be called whole, universal or variable life insurance, but the premise is that they combine life insurance with an investment portion that builds up a cash value. Many people who are buying life insurance like the idea of these cash value policies because they feel their premiums are building to something above and beyond the final payout. What they don't realize, though, is that for marginal added value, they're paying up to 1,000% more in fees. For the same amount of coverage, cash value polices can cost up to 10 times more than comparable term life policies. Because of the expensive nature of cash value insurance, many families can end up being under-insured. If you're shopping for life insurance, chances are agents and brokers will try to sell you a cash value policy, as they pay sizable commissions and bonuses to the seller. So be sure to ask for term life and save up to 10 times on your insurance costs.

BOTTOM LINE: Avoid all the confusion: buy pure term life insurance and spend up to 10 times less on premiums and get fully insured for your family's needs.

Start an Emergency Fund

An emergency fund is a stash of cash set aside in an accessible account, usually a high-interest savings account. Emergency needs vary from person to situation, but they usually involve an unforeseen event that requires an immediate sum of money. Having some funds tucked away for a rainy day can spare you from turning to credit cards, going into debt and paying high interest charges when times are tough. Keep in mind, though, that an emergency fund is not for buying a new pair of Jimmy Choo shoes, even if they are on sale! Here are some tangible reasons why you may need an emergency fund:

- **Illness:** If a long-term illness keeps you from working and earning money.
- **Job loss:** If you get laid off and cannot find work.
- **Natural disaster:** If your home and personal belongings are blown away in a storm.
- **Death:** If you lose a loved one.
- **Fire:** If your apartment burns to the ground and you need some replacement clothing before your insurance claim clears.
- **Car problems:** If your car breaks down on the highway and you need it towed from the off-ramp.
- **Busted water heater:** If your home is swimming in water and you need it fixed today.

These scenarios vary in hardship, but in each case some extra emergency money would be helpful.

How do you start building an emergency fund? I started my first emergency fund by socking away $25 every paycheque, or $50 a month. As I built a budget, paid off debts and cut variable spending, it became easier to save $100 to $250 a month. My thought is it's better to save a little than to save nothing at all.

A simple system to boost savings is to automatically move your money to an accessible (but not too accessible) high-interest savings account earmarked for emergencies. You will earn a little interest as your fund grows.

How much stashed cash do you need? This is a hard question to answer. A financial adviser once suggested I keep $3,000, while a savvy financial friend believed three to six months' worth of living expenses would keep me safe. The answer really depends on your living costs, financial situation and level of comfort in knowing you have some financial stores for just-in-case situations.

If you're blown away by these numbers, then start small with a little cash and slowly build. From my experience, it's very settling to know there is a little moolah set aside for a rainy day. ■

CHAPTER 4

Shopping

The reasons we shop can be as varied as our personalities. Some of us spend money in stores only out of pure necessity, while others approach shopping with as much zeal and fervour as an athlete training for the Olympics. Whether you're shopping for basic needs or fulfilling wants, changes to your shopping habits can have a huge impact on how much money you save.

Some shopping adjustments, like looking online for coupons, are simple habits to adopt and can quickly save you some dollars in the short term. Other lifestyle habits, such as shopping only with cash, are larger changes that may take some practice to adopt. Regardless of how you currently shop, there are ways to save money on your future purchases.

This past winter I put my own shopping habits to the test while looking for a pair of snowshoes to help me get around in the deep Canadian snow. The local big-box store stocked a pair that would have served me well, but after doing some quick research I found a better model online and at a lower price.

Finding a coupon for free shipping at one of my favourite deal-tracking websites sealed the sale, and I bought a better pair of snowshoes for far less money.

While finding a coupon and taking advantage of sales is ideal, there are times when paying full price for a quality, long-lasting item is not a bad idea. This was the case when I purchased a high-quality merino wool sweater, which wasn't the least expensive option in town. For the price of the wool sweater, I could have purchased two cheaper synthetic tops in the same store. But I opted to pay full price for the one wool sweater because I felt it would last a lot longer. This is an example of how I shopped with a preference for quality over quantity, and this tactic has served my pocketbook well over the years, saving me from replacing clothing and other items frequently. So keep in mind that many strategies will help you to stretch your shopping budget—both in the long and the short term.

Deciding what you want to buy is easy for most of us—maybe a bit too easy! But by following some straightforward tips on shopping, you can get both what you need and what you want—while saving money.

Buying Tactics

Before you hit the shops to spend some coin, arm yourself with these budget-saving tips to keep the most money in your pocket.

➤ **Don't waste money on brand names.** Don't believe the expensive marketing hype behind many brand-name products. Items carrying a brand are not necessarily better or worth the substantially higher price than the less advertised alternatives. Be wary of companies that spend lots of money on image-oriented advertising, as marketing costs big bucks and you're paying for that cost in the product. Save 10% to 50% by purchasing quality generic food, clothing, cleaning supplies, toiletries and kitchen supplies.

BOTTOM LINE: On a $75 cart of groceries, going generic will save you up to $37.50—cash in the bank on every shopping trip.

➤ **Ask for a discount.** Asking to pay less for a product or service sounds difficult, but it's not. Just be polite and ask, "Is this the best price you can offer me?" Finding a store manager can usually net good results immediately. Just by asking the question, I've walked away saving 10% to 15% on area rugs, mirrors, furniture and a camera. Offering to pay cash for an item rather than using plastic can often help too. Asking for a discount is free. Saving 10% with less than five minutes of work is time well spent.

BOTTOM LINE: Ask for a discount on everything you buy. You may just save a few bucks.

➤ **Barter to save money.** If you're parting with stuff you no longer want, then give the age-old practice of bartering a try. Generally, bartering is the trading of goods and services without the use of money. Check out the website

U-exchange.com to find like-minded people to trade such things as a camper for a vacation or to swap services like website building for a haircut. When contacting people sight unseen, don't agree to major trades without doing research first, and steer clear of gift card trades, as many experienced barterers have reported dubious issues with swapping goods for useless plastic.

BOTTOM LINE: Clean out your quality or unused clutter by bartering for goods and services you need, saving you from paying 100% of the cost.

➤ **Buy quality over quantity.** Developing a preference for buying fewer things of higher quality could save you thousands over your lifetime. When buying items like a sofa, a pair of pants, a washing machine or a coat, it makes sense to spend a bit more so that they last for several years. You may save a few bucks buying a cheaper coat, but you will also have to replace it sooner when the seams come apart. Spending more money on real wood furniture instead of manufactured sawdust may seem like a waste if the items look similar, but when core items can last decades and be handed down through generations, then consider it an investment over the longer term.

BOTTOM LINE: Always try to buy good-quality essential items instead of cheaper, less durable ones. This will save countless dollars over the long term. A $39 bookcase that lasts only a year isn't a steal compared with a $150 bookcase that lasts 15 years (or $10 per year).

➤ **Use your loyalty program points.** If you collect points from loyalty programs like Air Miles or Aeroplan, then be sure to redeem them. Loyalty program points are not like money in the bank—they don't earn interest and compound over time—so it makes little sense to hold on to them for years. Also be aware that loyalty program points can expire if you fail to continue collecting for a set number of days. Cash in your points as soon as you can to save your real money. Check out weekly deals and specials on the program's website for great rewards for fewer points.

BOTTOM LINE: Buying products and services with loyalty program points can save you from spending your real dollars. Just be sure to use your points before they expire.

➤ **Buy refurbished items.** Buying a refurbished laptop, vacuum cleaner or appliance can save you hundreds to thousands of dollars. Refurbished models are often items returned to the store for no reason, then tested at a factory to make sure they're in perfect working order. Defective or damaged parts are replaced and the unit is sold for a deep discount in retail stores and online. When looking to save on a refurbished product, be sure to buy only factory-certified items, which have been returned to and tested by the manufacturer. Factory-certified refurbished items must carry a full manufacturer's warranty to be worth your valuable dollars. Be wary of products labelled "recondi-tioned," as these may be used products that have been leased and then repaired by a retailer.

BOTTOM LINE: Buying refurbished electronics and appliances can save you hundreds and thousands of dollars if you shop around online. Ask retailers if they carry refurbished models on site to get the deal sooner.

➤ **Buy from wholesale superstores.** Go shopping at wholesale superstores like Costco and Sam's Club to pay 20% to 40% less over regular retail stores. In addition to saving lots of money, buying in bulk means you make fewer trips and can save on gas. But be wary of getting sucked into buying 10 litres of mayonnaise. It's not a good buy if your "great deal" ends up rotting in your fridge, leaving egg on your face. And comparison shop to make sure that your savings are worth the cost of membership. **BOTTOM LINE:** Shopping at wholesale superstores can save you 20% to 40% on food, clothing and household items over regular retail stores.

➤ **Shop at off-price department stores.** Check for deals at off-price department stores like Winners where brand-name clothing, footwear, bedding, furniture and housewares are available for 20% to 60% below regular department and specialty store prices. But before heading to the register with your fabulous finds, be sure to examine each item closely for damage, and watch out for factory seconds. **BOTTOM LINE:** Save 20% to 60% off brand-name items by shopping at off-price department stores.

➤ **Pass on extended warranties.** Don't buy extended warranties on inexpensive products like cameras and kitchen appliances. The only time a warranty makes sense is if a repair will devastate your budget. Warranties sold at the cash register earn retailers big bucks, costing you major bucks in added fees.

BOTTOM LINE: Pass on buying extended warranties on inexpensive products and save yourself from spending an extra $10 to $100 dollars. Pop that cash into your emergency fund instead so that you can cover any needed repairs—and watch your interest grow in the meantime.

➤ **Avoid buying on credit.** Only buy today what you can afford today, even if the item is on sale. Credit card interest charges can erode any advantage a sale item might have garnered. Instead, stick to shopping with the dollars you have today and start saving up for tomorrow's irresistible deals.

BOTTOM LINE: If you don't have the money to pay off your credit cards, avoid shopping even if the item is on sale. Credit interest charges cost you 15% to 20% a year and erode your savings.

➤ **Shop out of season.** Save some serious dollars by buying goods out of season. Buy winter boots in the spring, get wrapping paper after Christmas and buy a bike in the fall. Buying goods out of season means finding end-of-season sales, reductions and clear-outs, saving you as much as 75% off the ticket price.

BOTTOM LINE: Shop out of season to save up to 75%.

➤ **Buy used items through traditional sources.** Need some furniture, books, clothing or a car? Buying used goods not only saves on taxes but saves you from spending top dollar on retail pricing. Buying used items in excellent condition from traditional sources like garage sales, classified ads, friends and family can save you at least 50%. It may take time to find exactly what you're looking for, but given the savings, the time spent hunting is money in the bank.

BOTTOM LINE: Before hitting the shops, look for used household items in classified ads and at garage sales to save over 50%.

➤ **Buy used items online.** The Internet is a beautiful thing for bargain hunters looking for deals on used items. The Internet is open 24 hours a day and is an excellent resource for finding local people with used stuff to sell at rock-bottom prices. Sites like craigslist.ca, kijiji.ca and ebay.ca are amazing resources for finding everything you need, from a used kitchen table to baby gear for Junior. Be sure to find your city in the searches and deal only with local sellers to minimize the risks of dubious dealings. Buying locally also saves on shipping costs, which can defray the benefits of buying used.

BOTTOM LINE: Use Internet classified sites to find deals on used items, but stick to local sellers to prevent unsavoury dealings and to save on shipping.

➤ **Shop online using promotional codes.** When you're in the market to buy new merchandise, it's well worth your time to check out online retailers like Overstock.com or the websites of brick-and-mortar retailers like Sears.ca or Futureshop.ca. Many retailers offer deeper discounts online than in their storefronts, saving you anywhere from a few dollars to half of your purchase on some items. When shopping for new items online, always look for promotional codes before clicking "Buy" in your shopping cart. Sites like retailmenot.com and redflagdeals.com boast strong communities who post coupons and codes to save you bigger bucks on purchases in many categories, including travel, electronics, financial services, entertainment, apparel, automotive, housewares and food. Another great way to find money-saving promo codes is to type the desired retailer's name and then "coupon code" into your search engine. You may have to try several coupon codes before finding one that works—but you'll get lucky eventually, so be patient.

BOTTOM LINE: Find online promotional codes with sites retailmenot.com and redflagdeals.com and save up to 50% when ordering services or new merchandise online.

➤ **Don't pay for shipping.** Look for a free-shipping option when buying from an online store. Getting your items shipped for free could save you tens of dollars or a percentage off the total price on your order—so it pays to shop for shipping deals. Many online retailers offer free shipping when you buy up to a specified dollar amount in merchandise. If you aren't offered free shipping before checkout, then look for promotional codes through retailmenot.com and redflagdeals.com to cut on costs. Another creative method for saving on shipping is to order online from a store that also has a brick-and-mortar storefront and opt for in-store pickup—for free. Not only will you qualify for web-only discounts not offered in the store but you can get your merchandise much faster by picking it up in person. A friend of mine used this method to save $50 off the price of a DVD player by visiting the store in person and ordering the player using his cell phone web browser—he waited only a few minutes to pick up his package!

BOTTOM LINE: When shopping online, pick up merchandise in person to save on shipping charges. If the online retailer does not have a store, find promotional codes to save on shipping charges.

➤ **Search freecycle.org for free goods.** It's often said that one person's trash is another person's treasure. This is certainly the case with the popular free-goodies website called the Freecycle Network, an international community recycling project sharing usable goods for free. With the Freecycle Network, members post messages to local groups offering their used goods like furniture and clothing for free. If you find something you like or need, just message the owner and arrange a pickup! Joining and using Freecycle costs nothing, and you never know what you'll find by watching postings. Some members have found free kitchen cabinets, sports equipment and winter clothing for free. Shopping for other people's unwanted goods not only saves you huge dollars but reduces waste in landfills.

BOTTOM LINE: You could pick up a used patio set for free through the Freecycle Network. Visit freecycle.org to find the closest group in your area.

Selling Tactics

Take a look around your home and open sealed boxes, peek into the back of closets and dust off forgotten CDs. If you see things you haven't used in months or years, raise some funds and clear some space by selling your used stuff locally. There are lots of ways to make money from your quality clutter, from traditional garage sales to free online classified websites.

➤ **Sell your stuff the traditional way.** We see them most weekends in the summer: signs advertising neighbourhood garage sales. If you've got some stuff to sell, then hold a garage sale to unload your extras and make some money. Contact your neighbours and see if they too have saleable items and make it a street party to entice bigger crowds. If you're not into hanging out in your garage on Saturday, then place a classified ad in the local newspaper to reach a targeted community. Classifieds can start at $10 per ad, depending on what you're selling. If most of your used goods are gently worn shoes and brand-name clothing, then look in your area for consignment stores to sell your stuff. Consignment stores are generally second-hand shops that sell your goods while you retain ownership—until sold to a customer. Upon sale, the consignment shop earns a hefty commission ranging from 40% to 60% of the total. Despite the commission, consignment shops could be your best bet to recoup some money from items otherwise sitting around and collecting dust. Some money in your pocket is not a bad deal.

BOTTOM LINE: Sell your quality goods through newspaper classifieds, garage sales or via consignment shops to recoup at least 10% of the initial cost of your items.

➤ **Sell your stuff for free online.** If you've got stuff to sell and you're willing to write a description and take a good photo, then go online and hawk your wares for free on craigslist.ca or kijiji.ca. I've sold many items I no longer needed and recouped up to 60% of my purchase price by using these online classified sites targeting local buyers. Setting up an account is free, and the sites keep your email address hidden from prospective buyers until you initiate contact. Here are some points to consider when selling with online classifieds:

1. Before you start, search for listings advertising items similar to your own to get a feel for how much to charge for your item. Also take note of which product descriptions would entice you as a buyer and which ones just fall flat.

2. Post your classified ad with as many details and photos as possible. Save yourself from having to answer endless

emails requesting additional details by posting a complete advertisement at the get-go.

3. Be upfront with payment terms. If you want cash then state, "Cash only, please!" Be ready for cost-conscious people emailing you to haggle on price or barter for trades. If you're not willing to haggle or barter, then use the statement: "Item is priced as marked and no trades will be accepted."

4. Be prepared for people to email looking for you to ship your wares out of town. Save money by only selling to local residents. I've always included this line in my ads: "Local offers only." That ensures I can meet prospective buyers in person and collect payment in exchange for the item. Labelling your ad with the right geographical location may help as well. Also, if you do ship your goods, to be doubly safe, don't ship until you've received payment.

5. Prepare your items for showings by keeping them clean and presentable. Be prepared to answer questions on usage, age and warranties. If you're meeting with a stranger, arrange an appointment in a public place and bring a friend to be safe.

6. Stick to your price and don't feel disheartened if the deal falls through. The Internet is a big place, and it may take some time to connect your goods with the right buyer. If you're not getting much interest, consider rewriting your ad and posting new photos.

BOTTOM LINE: Selling your stuff online with free classifieds sites kijiji.ca or craigslist.ca can earn you extra cash from the clutter sitting in your closet. The amount of money you earn depends on the age, condition and desirability of the item.

➤ **Donate goods to those in need.** If selling your stuff is not an option, consider donating to a local charity or shelter or offer it through the Freecycle Network via freecycle.org. Giving away your unwanted things may just help someone in need and encourages neighbourhood recycling.

BOTTOM LINE: Rather than throw your items in the trash, donate them to organizations that help others in need. There isn't any financial incentive here unless you're moving, in which case cutting down on clutter also cuts down on costs.

PART TWO

Home Management

Adding up your bills and calculating how much you spend on energy costs, home maintenance charges and cleaning expenses may just shock you. It's amazing how the everyday costs of powering a television or cleaning your countertops can add up. In this section you'll learn about the power of saving on energy, the value of taking care of your space and the bucks to be saved with inexpensive baking soda—seriously! You may just feel inspired to turn down the heat by even one degree and think twice before throwing out your old toothbrush (and save hundreds in the process).

CHAPTER 5

Home Maintenance

Regular home maintenance is money in the bank. It sounds counterintuitive, spending on repairs to become richer, but it's true. Inspecting your home on a regular basis and maintaining it with care is the best way to protect your investment and to prevent larger problems from breaking the bank in the future.

Getting into the habit of seasonal maintenance is quick and easy when you know what to look for. Just set aside some time each month, season or year to check for cracks, peer into vents and put a stop to costly problems before they occur. In many cases inspecting and maintaining your home is free, and the minimal cost of small fixes is a smart investment in the overall health of what is probably your largest investment.

➤ **Replace batteries in carbon monoxide detectors and smoke alarms.** Checking the batteries regularly in your smoke alarms and carbon monoxide detectors is free and could save you from losing everything you own in a home fire. Batteries are an inexpensive way to protect your home and loved ones. Many local fire departments recommend changing them twice a year to match the spring forward and fall back of daylight savings time.

BOTTOM LINE: Buying replacement batteries for $2 to $5 could save you from having to spend thousands to repair home and property damage and may save you some dollars on your home insurance costs.

➤ **Check pressure in fire extinguishers.** It takes only two minutes once a year to check the pressure gauge of your fire extinguisher. Fire extinguishers are sold by the weight of the active ingredient used to put out fires. A small extinguisher, weighing 2 pounds, costs $25, while a larger one, weighing 6 pounds, costs $70. The minimum recommended size for a kitchen unit is 2.5 pounds, although a 5-pound unit is ideal in case of larger fires. Get an extinguisher with a metal nozzle, not plastic—fire equipment service companies often only recharge metal-nozzle units. If your extinguisher requires more charge, look online for a local fire equipment service company to do the job so an efficient way to put out fires is always right at hand.

BOTTOM LINE: A fire extinguisher may cost $50 to purchase and $10 to recharge, but when kept in your kitchen it could prevent thousands of dollars in damage.

➤ **Clean eavestroughs and downspouts.** Preventing water damage is essential to keeping your home's foundation solid. One of the biggest culprits in causing water damage is faulty eavestroughs and downspouts. The eavestroughs on many homes can become clogged with leaves and other debris, preventing rainwater and melting snow from draining away from your house. Cleaning your eaves in the fall and spring will keep the rain and winter runoff from spilling over the edge of the trough onto the ground, where a buildup of moisture can seep into the basement. Simply hop up on a steady ladder and scoop any debris into a compost bag.

BOTTOM LINE: This two-hour task will cost you 30 cents in bags but can save you tens of thousands of dollars by keeping your foundation from cracking.

➤ **Inspect water pipes throughout the house for leaks.** A small drip can quickly turn into a major leak causing significant damage. Leaks can cause moisture buildup, leading to mould—which is very expensive to get rid of. Check your water pipes and drainpipes for drips and other signs of leakage at least once a year. Look under every sink, inspect shutoff valves and look at the U-joint of each drain. Running hot and cold water when inspecting each pipe helps to identify leaks in shutoff valves of sinks, toilets and around the U-joints of drains. Closely monitor ceilings of each room located beneath bathrooms for water damage.

BOTTOM LINE: Checking pipes is free. A small leak is cheaper to repair (a plumber may charge a few hundred dollars) than a larger problem causing mould and costing thousands.

➤ **Clean or replace furnace and air-conditioning filters.** Changing your furnace or air-conditioner filter monthly during the heating and cooling seasons will keep your home's air clean, your house dust free and your energy costs low. Routinely changing filters means less vacuuming and cleaning, improves your health and extends the life of your furnace by reducing strain on the system.

BOTTOM LINE: A basic paper filter costs $3 while a high-performance filter runs $35, a small price to pay to save hundreds in improved energy efficiency.

➤ **Check your basement for moisture.** You need to know if your basement is leaking. Moisture in the basement can cause mould and considerable structural damage to your home. Do a visual inspection every fall, looking inside for damp areas on walls, mould growth or smells, mineral stains on exposed concrete, cracks in concrete and discoloured or warped vinyl flooring. If you have an older home, it might be helpful to take a picture of your basement walls each fall to compare for new stains and other problems. Check outside for ground sloping toward your home and for damaged or clogged eavestroughs. If you suspect moisture, hire a contractor for a few hundred dollars to test your basement using a moisture meter. Be sure you hire a professional and be mindful of possible conflicts of interest if the contractor quotes you a price for fixing the problem.

BOTTOM LINE: Repairing a small moisture problem in your basement before it becomes a big one could save you from getting soaked. If you notice moisture issues, hire a contractor for a few hundred dollars to suggest a solution.

➤ **Get your heating, ventilation, air conditioning and fireplace professionally inspected.** Natural Resources Canada recommends homeowners get yearly inspections from a heating, ventilating and air conditioning (HVAC) specialist to check heating and cooling systems. A gas furnace should be serviced once a year to inspect exhaust piping, to test the heat exchanger and to inspect the safety controls and fan in the unit.

BOTTOM LINE: Professional HVAC inspections cost about $150, while the cost of doing nothing could add up to a few thousand dollars in more extensive repairs. An inefficient furnace will cost you in higher heating bills; a carbon monoxide leak could cost you a loved one.

➤ **Replace damaged, cracked or frayed electrical cords throughout your home.** Walk around your home once a year and inspect all extension cords and electrical cords. Look for cracks in outer insulation, especially near the plugs, and feel the cord to see if the insulation is getting brittle. Keep a close eye on heavily used extension cords, such as on your vacuum cleaner. When buying replacement appliance cords, be sure the new cord is rated for a wattage equal to or higher than the cord it replaces. If the appliance has a removable cord, it may be possible to find a replacement cord for under $15. If the damaged cord is wired into an inexpensive small appliance, consult a small appliance repair professional to see if a replacement cord can save the unit for less than replacement cost.

BOTTOM LINE: Replacing worn electrical and extension cords costs $5 to $15 and can prevent a devastating fire that costs you thousands in damages.

➤ **Clear debris from air conditioner coolant coils.** It costs nothing to remove dirt and garden debris from the coils of your air-conditioning unit. Debris clogging your air conditioner's coils makes the unit work harder, costing you in increased energy consumption.

BOTTOM LINE: Clearing leaves and dirt from your air conditioner is free and can cut your energy costs by up to 5%.

CHAPTER 6

Energy

Saving money on energy is easier than you think. Our continual use of heating and cooling, electricity and water present numerous opportunities to save money in our homes with just the flick of a switch. Statistics Canada reports that in 2007 the average Canadian family spent $2,203 on water and energy alone. By simply turning off unused lights and turning down the heat by just a bit, many homes could save at least 5% on their energy costs, resulting in an additional $100 or more a year.

Spending money on more efficient electronic devices and appliances can also save you big energy bucks over the long term. If you're in the market for a washing machine or a TV, consider buying products with certification labels like ENERGY STAR to maximize savings.

Spending even bigger money on structural changes may pay off in the end. If you are in a position to renovate your home or are looking for ways to improve your energy efficiency, find out about federal and provincial programs that help Canadian families make these changes. One such program is the Canadian government's ecoENERGY Retrofit grant program; for $150 a certified energy adviser visits your home and measures your energy consumption and efficiency. Based on these measurements, the adviser provides written recommendations for what you can specifically do to decrease your energy costs. After meeting with an energy adviser in my own home, I found ways to save money by sealing the attic and insulating pipes and I even qualified for $1,600 in energy rebates by replacing my old oil furnace with an ENERGY STAR electric heating system.

Check out the ecoACTION website (ecoaction.gc.ca) to find an energy adviser and to learn how to qualify for energy rebates in your province. You may be surprised by how making small, inexpensive changes to your home can add up to big dollars saved.

Heating and Cooling

Heating and cooling your home accounts for almost half of your energy bill, making it the single largest energy expense for most Canadians. Whether you rent or own, you can take inexpensive steps to reduce your heating and cooling bills and make your home more energy efficient. Here are some tips for adding some cool cash to your wallet while keeping yourself seasonally comfortable.

Heating

➤ **Turn down the heat.** For every degree you set your thermostat lower, you save up to 5% on your annual heating costs. A single degree of less heat can translate into hundreds saved a year. If you want to be very energy efficient, try to get down to a setting of 18°C—but start by moving down one degree at a time. Taking a warm woolly sweater from your wardrobe or snuggling into bed under an extra blanket is free and allows you to keep your room temperature lower.

BOTTOM LINE: Bundling up and turning down the thermostat can save you 5% on your heating bill over the year. For the average Canadian family this can add up to $100 each year.

➤ **Install a programmable thermostat.** Installing a programmable thermostat to automatically turn down the heat at night and when you're away can save you hundreds a year. A programmable thermostat costs as little as $30 at most hardware stores. Check your furnace manual to see which thermostats are compatible with your heating system. If you're not ready to spend the money on a new programmable thermostat, then try setting your thermostat to 16°C before you go to bed at night and again before leaving the house for the day. One month's worth of diligent monitoring should just about pay for the new thermostat.

BOTTOM LINE: A programmable thermostat has a one-time cost of $30 and can save you up to 10% on your energy bill.

➤ **Replace your furnace with a high-efficiency system.**
Got an old oil, electric or gas furnace burning through
your energy dollars? Consider replacing your old heating
system with a new ENERGY STAR furnace. If you qualify
under the Government of Canada's ecoENERGY Retrofit grant program, you could see up to a $1,600 rebate.
Contact a certified energy adviser before overhauling your
heating system though, to find out if you qualify and to
see if the expense is worth the savings.
**BOTTOM LINE: A new furnace could set you back $5,000 but
gain you $1,600 in federal rebates—plus hundreds in energy
savings each year.**

➤ **Shut vents in unused rooms.** Not every room in your
home needs to be kept piping warm. By shutting heating
vents in empty or less frequented rooms, you can save
money by not heating them. Closing heating vents in the
winter is free and can save you up to 5% in heating costs.
Just be sure to keep an eye open for condensation forming
on windows in cooler rooms, as this could cause mould.
**BOTTOM LINE: Reducing the heated area of your home could
save you 5% on your heating bill.**

Cooling

➤ **Turn up the temperature.** Consider embracing summer by turning your air conditioner one to two degrees
warmer and watch your energy savings add up. Every

degree warmer you set your air conditioner equals up to 5% in energy savings.

BOTTOM LINE: Being one degree warmer can save you up to 5% on your energy bill, which on an average electricity bill of $85 a month saves up to $50 a year.

➤ **Use a fan instead of an air conditioner.** Consider running a fan to circulate cooling air flow throughout your home in the summer. Not using a central air conditioner or a window-mounted unit can cut your cooling bill by up to 90%. While floor fans can be great for cooling a small space, ceiling fans are the most effective for moving air in a larger room. If your home is blazing hot, try sleeping in the basement for free to cool your costs.

BOTTOM LINE: Passing on an air conditioner altogether and running a fan can save up to 90% on your cooling costs.

➤ **Install a programmable thermostat.** Running an air conditioner on full when the house is empty all day is a phenomenal waste of money. Install a programmable thermostat for about $30 to save up to 20% on your cooling costs. Set the temperature to 24°C or higher to maximize savings while at home and set the temperate from 5 to 10 degrees warmer for when you're away.

BOTTOM LINE: Install a programmable thermostat to save you up to 20% on your cooling costs.

➤ **Install your air conditioner in the shade.** If you are installing a central air conditioner outdoors, try to situate it on the north side of your house in the shade. A shaded air conditioner stays cooler and operates more efficiently, saving you 5% in energy costs.

BOTTOM LINE: An air conditioner located in the shade could decrease your energy bill by 5%, and it costs you zero dollars to install it on the north side of your home.

➤ **Plant a tree.** Planting trees on the south side of your home can help reduce summer cooling costs. Deciduous trees, which lose their leaves in the fall, provide ample shade in the summer, keeping your home cooler and letting more warming light through in the winter. Planting trees around your home can have the added bonus of increasing your property value.

BOTTOM LINE: The price of a single deciduous tree can start at $50 and can pay for itself in energy savings and increased property value.

Air Leaks

Air leaks caused by poor insulation, drafty windows or poorly sealed doors can contribute to an unhealthy and cold home environment. There are ways to increase the environmental comfort of your home while increasing your energy savings. You may even qualify for an energy rebate with the Government of Canada's ecoENERGY Retrofit grant program by following these tips.

Insulation

➤ **Add more insulation to your attic.** Adding insulation to the attic of an older home can keep you warmer in the winter and cooler in the summer. Going from 8 inches of fibreglass insulation to 16 inches could also mean you qualify for a $300 rebate from the Government of Canada's ecoENERGY program.

BOTTOM LINE: A well-insulated attic can save you 10% to 15% in energy costs.

➤ **Make the attic hatch airtight.** Pick up some weatherstripping and a piece of foam board insulation at the hardware store to get started on this DIY fix. Use the weatherstripping to seal all four edges and then cut the foam board to size and attach to the back with adhesive, making sure the attic hatch still opens easily.

BOTTOM LINE: The whole job will take you 15 minutes, cost you $20 and save you up to 5% in energy costs.

➤ **Seal electrical outlets.** Electrical outlets can be a sizable source of air leaks in your home. Outlets on exterior walls are the biggest leaky culprits, costing you 2% to 5% in energy loss. Increase your energy efficiency by removing the outlet covers (turn off the electricity flow first) and insulating all electrical outlets with a CSA-approved foam gasket. Gaskets cost 20 cents each but save you up to 5% in energy costs. For maximum savings, seal unused outlets with childproof plastic plugs.

BOTTOM LINE: The total bill for insulating your electrical

outlets with foam gaskets and childproof plugs is under $20 and can save you 5% in energy costs.

➤ **Close seldom used fireplaces.** Fireplace dampers rarely fit snugly and cost you in heat loss. If you don't use your fireplace regularly, consider installing a removable plywood cover that can be insulated, weather-stripped and sealed with a gasket. Spending $50 to properly seal your fireplace creates a more comfortable living area and can save on heating costs. Just be sure to remove the insulating cover when it's time to build a fire!

BOTTOM LINE: Insulate and seal your rarely used fireplace for $50 and save up to 30% on your energy bill.

➤ **Seal cracks and crevices with polyurethane foam.** A spray can of expandable polyurethane foam can fill most small cracks and crevices throughout your home. Use foam around an unfinished basement to plug cold, drafty areas and to insulate cable boxes and cracks around the exterior of your home. Some homes have an exterior faucet that can benefit from insulation. Insulating these seemingly small open spaces can save you 5% on your energy bills. Be sure to keep the foam away from heated areas and open flames like your furnace and chimney.

BOTTOM LINE: A can of expandable polyurethane foam costs $8 and could lower your energy costs by 5%.

Windows and Doors

➤ **Weather-strip and caulk windows and doors.** Air leaks around windows and doors can significantly increase your heating and cooling costs. Weatherstripping and silicone caulking are an inexpensive way of stopping drafts from entering your home. Check annually and replace weatherstripping as needed. Use silicone to seal cracks around the outside of all door and window frames.

BOTTOM LINE: A tube of caulking costs $5 and weatherstripping can run $5 to $10 per window or door. Energy savings can add up to 10% each year.

➤ **Apply plastic film to winterize windows.** Make your windows airtight by applying a thin plastic film over the window and frame and fastening with double-sided adhesive tape. For about $30, enough plastic film and tape can be purchased to cover most windows in a home. A more expensive insulating kit using acrylic plastic sheets costs $50 to $100 but can be reused for several years. Winterizing windows with plastic film is great for renters because it's inexpensive and impermanent but can cut expenses if you pay for heat.

BOTTOM LINE: Using a plastic film over your windows in the winter costs you $30 to $100 (depending on the kit) but can save you 20% to 30% in energy expenses.

➤ **Replace older windows.** Windows in older homes can be a significant source of heat loss, increasing energy costs by up to 30%. New windows can cost upwards of $1,000 each, but rebates are available through the Government of Canada's ecoENERGY Retrofit grant program. Consult with a certified energy adviser to qualify for rebates of up to $60 per window. If it's too much of a stretch to spring for new windows now, use as many of the other strategies as possible to lower your energy bills and then set aside your savings in a Tax-Free Savings Account (TFSA) or a standard high-interest account for a window fund. You'll be surprised how it adds up in just a few years.

BOTTOM LINE: New windows are expensive at upwards of $1,000 each but can lower your heating and cooling costs by 30%. As a bonus, new windows can also increase the value of your home when you are ready to sell.

➤ **Hang drapes and blinds.** Use your existing heavy insulated drapes to save you 8% to 15% in heating costs. To get warmer for free, close your drapes or blinds at night and on shaded sides of the home while opening them on sunny days. Drapes can also keep your home cooler in the summer by shading your home from the hot afternoon sunlight. Heavy insulating drapes can cost hundreds to thousands of dollars depending on the number of windows and the size of your home.

BOTTOM LINE: Existing drapes and blinds can be opened or closed for free to keep your home warmer and cut your energy costs by 8% to 15%.

➤ **Close doors in rooms not frequently used.** Keeping both exterior and interior doors tightly shut and avoiding frequent in and out traffic costs nothing and lowers your energy costs. Use padded door runners or rolled towels to help reduce drafts under doorways.

BOTTOM LINE: Closing doors and placing a rolled towel under doorways is free and can save you 2% on your energy bill.

Electricity

We all need electricity to light our homes and power our appliances. Despite this considerable need to draw on hydro, you can cut your costs by hundreds, even thousands, a year by adopting frugal and easy energy-saving habits. From how you light your home to choosing the more energy-efficient electronic devices, here are numerous ways to add money to your pocket without feeling shocked by drastic change.

Lighting

➤ **Turn off lights.** Keeping your lights on when no one is in the room is costing you. Natural Resources Canada says it costs between $200 and $250 to light the average home each year. A 100-watt bulb left on for an hour costs 1 cent. But 300 watts of unused lights left on for three hours each day costs $11 a year.

BOTTOM LINE: Save $11 a year by turning off unused lights for three hours each day.

➤ **Install light dimmers around your home.** Dimming a lamp by 25% increases light bulb life by four times and saves you 20% on electricity costs. Dimmer prices start at $10 each and can go up to $80.

BOTTOM LINE: Inexpensive dimmers cost $10 each and are a frugal way to save about $50 a year on the average electricity bill, while extending bulb life.

➤ **Install a motion sensor outdoors.** Installing a motion sensor outdoors can serve as a security light *and* save you money. Leaving a 100-watt bulb burning for 24 hours costs 25 cents a day. Switching to a motion sensor costs $50 and saves you $90 a year by only switching on when needed.

BOTTOM LINE: If you install a motion sensor it will pay for itself in just over six months and then go on to save you $90 each year.

➤ **Replace incandescent bulbs with compact fluorescent lamps (CFLs).** At $2 to $5 each, compact fluorescent lamps cost five times more than conventional bulbs but use 25% of the electricity and last 8 to 15 times longer.

BOTTOM LINE: Switching to compact fluorescent lamps may cost you $100 in the short term but saves you 75% on lighting costs over the longer term.

➤ **Make use of natural light.** Open the drapes and let the sun shine in. Using natural daylight over electricity costs you nothing and saves on energy. Also, choosing to paint rooms in lighter colours and opening blinds can brighten your living space. Using natural sunlight and switching lights off during the day can save you hundreds of dollars a year.

BOTTOM LINE: Using natural light in place of five 60-watt bulbs for eight hours each day saves you $11 a year.

Appliances and Electronics

➤ **Turn off electronic devices.** Turning off your unused electrical devices like gaming consoles and computers is an easy way to save electricity. By turning on your computer only when needed for three hours each day rather than running it continuously, you can save up to $75 a year.

BOTTOM LINE: Turn off electrical devices when they're not in use and save hundreds a year.

➤ **Pull the plug on standby costs.** Plugged-in electronics are expensive because they continue to draw power to light up clocks, supply chargers and be on standby. This standby power can contribute to 10% of wasted and expensive energy loss. If you need a reminder, leave a note beside your electronic devices to unplug them.

BOTTOM LINE: Unplug these power-drawing devices and save a whopping 10% on energy costs each year.

➤ **Use a surge protector.** To save money while keeping your electronic devices plugged in, consider buying a surge protector for $5 to $20. Surge protectors can be switched off while electronic devices are plugged in, thus reducing standby power consumption. Using a surge protector to fully switch off your home entertainment system when not in use can save you $5 to $10 a year.

BOTTOM LINE: Use a surge protector to limit standby power waste and save you hundreds a year.

Water

Heating water is the second largest drain on your energy bill. By using inexpensive hot water saving strategies you can save considerable cash whether you rent an apartment or own a home.

➤ **Turn water temperature down.** Turning down your water heater's temperature to 60°C is easy and free. For every 10 degrees you decrease the tank's temperature you save 3% to 5% on your energy bill. You won't notice the difference because the hot water you use is at a much lower temperature than 60°C.

BOTTOM LINE: Reduce your water heater temperature to 60°C to save 3% to 5% on your energy costs.

➤ **Fix leaky taps.** A leaking hot water tap slowly drips your money down the drain. Seek a professional plumber to plug the leak or replace the gasket in the tap yourself. Because some leaks can waste enough water to fill a bathtub in a few days, it's wise to stop the drips and save some cash.

BOTTOM LINE: A leaky hot water tap can be fixed with a $1 gasket and save you $50 a year on energy costs. Consult a professional plumber for a few hundred dollars to solve more complicated issues sooner.

➤ **Insulate hot water pipes.** Keep the water hot for less by installing insulating sleeves on the hot water pipes in your home. Special foam insulation pieces can be purchased at a hardware store for 30 cents a foot. Start by covering the pipes near the hot water tank and work your way out to all easily accessible pipes. Be sure the insulation is a safe distance from any open flame or other source of ignition.

BOTTOM LINE: Pipe insulation costs $10 to $20 per home and can save you $50 a year.

➤ **Install a solar water heater.** Adding a solar water heater to your traditional water heater can add up to significant long-term savings. A solar water heater uses collector panels in which water is warmed by the sun; you save money because it doesn't cost so much to heat the water in your water heater. Professional systems cost around $5,000 and qualify for an ecoENERGY Retrofit grant. A home-built do-it-yourself solar water system costs under $1,000.

BOTTOM LINE: A homemade solar water heater costs $1,000 and can save you up to $300 per year, while professional systems cost $5,000 and can qualify for $1,600 in government energy grants.

CHAPTER 7

Cleaning

Cleaning our homes has become a multi-billion-dollar brand-name business. Between super-specialized cleaners marketed to help remove grime from the northwest corner of the shower and disposable options convincing us it's possible to have a sparkling house without an ounce of effort, there are hundreds of products designed not only to clean our homes but to clean out our wallets. But keeping your home clean doesn't need to be an expensive endeavour. Many cleaning products can be replaced or enhanced with items you probably already have around the house at a fraction of the cost. All it takes is a little bit of elbow grease and some common kitchen staples to clean regular spills and wash the dirt away.

I've been using simple, frugal and effective methods to clean my bathroom, kitchen, windows and floors for years. At first, I missed that "clean smell" that comes from using commercial products, but the more I cleaned the way my grandmother had, the more I realized that clean doesn't have a smell—and I was paying big bucks for that artificial lemon whiff and exposing my family to unnecessary harsh chemicals at the same time. This chapter is packed with cheap and natural solutions to help you save money not only at the store but over time as well, because cleaning your home on a regular basis helps to maintain the value of your investment and reduces the need to replace items because of soils and stains.

Cleansers

Replacing your brand-name household cleaners with inexpensive kitchen staples like vinegar, baking soda and liquid dishwashing soap can save you hundreds of dollars a year, and at the same time can protect your home surfaces from abrasive cleansers and strong chemicals.

➤ **Make your own glass cleaner.** Buying a reusable spray bottle for $3 and mixing your own glass-cleaning solution containing 1 part white vinegar and 1 part water saves you at least $25 a year over brand-name glass cleaners. Using vinegar and water to clean glass surfaces, mirrors and windows also reduces the number of harsh chemicals in your home. A 4-litre bottle of generic white vinegar costs only $1.50 and can last for months.
BOTTOM LINE: Making your own glass cleaner is environmentally friendly and saves you at least $25 a year. If you have an old spray bottle, refill it when it's empty and save $3, which is how much a new one would cost.

Home Cleaning Supplies Checklist

- ☐ Mild liquid dishwashing cleanser
- ☐ Baking soda paste
- ☐ Vinegar glass cleaner
- ☐ Reusable spray bottle
- ☐ Lint-free microfibre towels
- ☐ Quality rubber gloves
- ☐ Toilet scrub brush
- ☐ Sink scrub brush
- ☐ Used toothbrushes
- ☐ Sponge mop head with towels

➤ **Use baking soda to deodorize, remove stains and to scrub tough grime away.** Go beyond using baking soda for deodorizing your refrigerator and freezer by using this inexpensive cleaning marvel for tough dirt around your home. Replacing your arsenal of brand-name kitchen, bathroom and specialty cleaners with a big box of generic baking soda could save you hundreds of dollars a year. Baking soda can be used for scrubbing without scratching surfaces and is safe for removing stains from dishes, countertops, sinks and toilet bowls. Baking soda can also remove tough grease and buildup in ovens and on stovetops: scrub using a paste made by mixing 3 parts warm water and 1 part baking soda. The best deals on baking soda can be found at animal feed stores, where a 10 kg bag sells for 50 cents per kilogram. Baking soda bought at feed stores is not baking quality and is coarser than retail brands, but the price for cleaning cannot be beat when compared with brands sold in grocery stores at $5 per kilogram.

BOTTOM LINE: Replace your brand-name household cleaners with baking soda—not only will you save hundreds of dollars a year, but you will also protect your family from exposure to harsh chemicals. Buy baking soda at animal feed stores—it's 90% cheaper than at grocery stores.

➤ **Remove dried spills with diluted liquid dishwashing soap.**
Make an inexpensive all-purpose cleaner by mixing 1 cup of water with 1 tablespoon of generic liquid dishwashing soap in a $3 reusable spray bottle. Use this cleaner to spot-clean dried spills and remove greasy fingerprints throughout your home and on countertops and wood surfaces. Generic dish-washing soap costs only $2 per 950 mL, so diluting it with water and spraying with a bottle costs just pennies a week, saving you a bundle on brand-name cleaners in a year.

BOTTOM LINE: Cleaning with generic liquid dishwashing soap diluted with water in a reusable spray bottle costs pennies a week and saves you dozens of dollars a year.

➤ **Eliminate soap scum with lemon juice and white vinegar.**
Make a simple mixture of 1 cup white vinegar and the juice from half a lemon to remove soap scum from bathtubs and mineral deposits from sinks and faucets. Soak an old hand towel in this acidic mixture and cover deposits or residue for

several hours, then scrub. Vinegar is economical at $1.50 per 4-litre bottle and lemons can cost $1 for four.

BOTTOM LINE: Remove expensive and harsh soap scum–dissolving chemicals from your home and save hundreds a year by mixing lemon juice with vinegar. Scrubbing dirt and grime is free.

➤ **Clean wood, linoleum and tile flooring with vinegar and water.** For wood floors finished with polyurethane, linoleum surfaces and tiles, mop with a mix of 1 part vinegar with 1 part warm water. Vinegar costs $1.50 per 4-litre bottle and saves you hundreds on brand-name flooring cleaners. The vinegar cuts through grime and leaves a fresh scent throughout your home.

BOTTOM LINE: Clean your flooring for hundreds of dollars less by mixing vinegar with warm water.

➤ **Wipe up spills while they are fresh.** Spills in the kitchen and dirt in the doorway are always easier to clean when fresh. Attending to everyday grime sooner costs you far less in cleaning detergents; a hand towel and some elbow grease is all it takes to keep surfaces fresh and clean. Proper and regular cleaning also maintains the value of your home and protects the investment in your possessions, making your belongings last longer.

BOTTOM LINE: Wiping up spills immediately is free and costs you nothing in cleaning supplies. Regular cleaning and maintenance protects the investment in your home and belongings and reduces replacement costs by making things last longer.

Cleaning Tools

The tools you choose to clean your home with can save you money over time. Tools like reusable microfibre cloths and old toothbrushes are not only better for your budget but can be healthier for your household environment as well.

➤ **Use elbow grease and a good pair of rubber gloves.** A good pair of reusable rubber gloves can last for weeks and makes a great cleaning partner for a little bit of elbow grease. Gloves and elbow grease can save you from spending hundreds on corrosive chemicals to remove stubborn grime. Be sure to hang your gloves to dry to prevent mould and mildew growth from eating into your savings.
BOTTOM LINE: A pair of quality rubber gloves costs $2 to $5 and saves you hundreds on grime-removing corrosive chemicals.

➤ **Use an old toothbrush to get into hard-to-clean places.** Used toothbrushes can be recycled for cleaning throughout your home for free. Frayed bristles are a perfect match for faucets, tile grout, light switches and cabinet hardware. Toothbrushes are also excellent for cleaning calcium buildup in kettles or road grime on bike chains.
BOTTOM LINE: Replacing your toothbrush regularly is good for your dental health and it costs you nothing to reuse it as a cleaning tool throughout your home.

➤ **Pass on paper towels and use microfibre cloths.**
Microfibre cloths are woven from very fine synthetic fibres and are perfect for dusting, polishing, wiping and mopping. These soft and reusable cloths save you money because they are effective at cleaning delicate surfaces like computer monitors, they are machine washable and they don't require costly cleaning solutions to remove grime. Microfibre cloths come in a range of sizes and weights with varying loop sizes, and can cost as little as $5. Save on expensive endless rolls of paper towels by buying a bunch of microfibre cloths and washing them regularly. They can last years, save you hundreds of dollars and are a better option for our forests.

BOTTOM LINE: The average Canadian family uses two rolls of paper towels each week, at $2.19 per roll. That adds up to $188.34 per year, enough to pay for over 35 reusable, multipurpose microfibre towels!

➤ **Wash and reuse your Swiffer dusters.** The popular Swiffer brand of dusters and mops will cost you around $10 for a 32-pack refill, and each one can last for several cleanings. Extend the use of this handy electrostatic dusting and mopping tool by washing your dusters and mop heads in a laundry bag. Not only will you reduce the garbage created but you will save big. Alternatively, use a microfibre towel in place of the refillable sheet and save even more on mopping and dusting costs.

BOTTOM LINE: Swiffer brand dusters and mops are useful for cleaning throughout your home, so extend their use by

washing them in a laundry bag and save $20 to $30 a year. Use a microfibre cloth in place of the refillable sheet and save even more.

➤ **Maintain and save on your vacuum cleaner.** A quality vacuum can cost over $1,000 for the highly marketed models. To save hundreds on this important cleaning tool, avoid buying the top model in a series. Going up a model often buys you more attachments and features, but because vacuums from the same manufacturers tend to have the same motor and parts, you're getting the same unit for hundreds more. Maintaining your vacuum today will also save you from having to pay for repairs in the future. Always replace the bag before it gets too full—efficiency decreases as the bag fills. Ideally, replace the bag before it is three-quarters full.

BOTTOM LINE: Buy a quality middle-range vacuum cleaner and avoid spending hundreds more on the top-end unit with the same motor and parts. Maintain your vacuum by replacing bags before they are full and picking up sharp and awkward objects to protect the motor.

Make Your Own Machine-Washable Mop Head

Save $30 by making your own reusable, washable mop head. All you need is an old towel and the handle from an old sponge mop (like the Atlantic Bee mop). Fold up the towel into a thick pad and use the mechanism in the mop handle to clamp and secure the towel. For larger jobs, it's a good idea to keep a stack of several old towels on hand or cut an old large towel into sections. When you're done, toss all of the used towels into the laundry and wash them, separated from your other laundry, for the next cleaning day. ∎

PART THREE

Room by Room

When you walk around the rooms in your home, can you spot where to save? Can you see the power of compound interest when you sit on your sofa or see the savings when pouring laundry detergent? In this section I'll lead you around your living spaces and show you the endless opportunities to save additional dough in the kitchen, bedrooms, bathroom, on gas in your car and when planting a garden outside. Join millions of keener beaners by soaking dried beans, throw frugally fabulous kids' birthday parties, sleep better at night on affordable bedding and learn how to get your food for free by watching the price scanner. The tips in this section are fun to use, easy to follow and will make you wealthier, healthier, and wiser.

CHAPTER 8

Kitchen

Eating is an expensive fact of life. With three meals a day plus snacks and goodies, the cost of buying and preparing food is considerable and is not getting any cheaper. The average Canadian spends over 10% of their yearly expenses on food, and this doesn't account for dining in restaurants or ordering takeout meals. But despite the obvious need to eat, shopping for food and feeding your family doesn't have to be a financial strain.

Because decisions in the kitchen affect both your pocketbook and your waistline, some simple planning is all that's needed to maximize your savings without sacrificing your health. In fact, the majority of frugal meal choices favour the healthiest of foods, a win-win situation.

For example, my personal preference is to pass on expensive brand-name packaged foods and eat "frugalicious" food. Frugalicious is a word I coined to describe foods that are frugal, delicious and healthy—fruits, vegetables, lean meats, legumes, nuts and beans that pack a nutritional punch without knocking out your wallet. When bought in bulk and prepared at home, frugalicious foods stretch your dining dollar and feed a family for far less.

This chapter shows you how to save money by finding your own frugalicious foods and by making other simple adjustments in your kitchen. By making a few adaptations, it's easy to save money while eating a healthy, balanced diet.

➤ Get your food for free by watching the price scanner.

Mistakes on electronic price scans are common at the grocery store. The U.S. Federal Trade Commission has found that errors occur in 1 out of every 32 regularly priced items. Errors are more common on sale items, with 1 out of 28 items being overcharged to consumers. Watch as your items are scanned at the checkout and you could save many dollars per month and even score free food. The Retail Council of Canada has a Code of Practice for scanner accuracy that states, "If the scanned price of a qualifying item at the checkout of a participating store is higher than the price displayed in the store—or advertised by the store—the lower price will be honoured. If the correct price of the product is $10 or less, the retailer will give the product to the customer for free. If the correct price of the product is higher than $10, the retailer will give the customer $10 off the corrected price." See the Retail Council of Canada website (retailcouncil.org) for the list of participating stores in your area.

BOTTOM LINE: Watch as your groceries are scanned at the

checkout and verify that prices are accurate. If you see an error, don't be afraid to ask the cashier to give you the item for free.

➤ **Make a grocery list.** Ever come home from the supermarket without having bought anything to eat? It's not hard to do when you consider all the marketing displays and distractions at the grocery store. Food marketers pay mega-moolah for shelf space and want to catch your eye and tap your wallet when you're shopping for dinner. To save you hundreds or thousands in impulse buys, go through your pantry before hitting the supermarket and make a shopping list. Having a list with you when you go shopping not only saves time but reminds you what foods to buy and what meals to make and steers you clear of impulse purchases. Writing a shopping list is free and can help you plan menus for your breakfasts, lunches and dinners, saving you even more money from costly takeout meals and restaurants bills. You might even save on gas by being super-organized because you won't need to make a second trip!

BOTTOM LINE: Make a free grocery list and buy only the foods you need for breakfast, lunch and dinner. Even if you save only $10 on impulse buys each week, making a list can really pay off—to the tune of $520 a year.

➤ **Skip the supermarket aisles and shop around the edges.** The perimeter of your supermarket is stocked with the most healthful and frugalicious foods; items like fresh produce, dairy, bulk foods, meats, organics and frozen vegetables are ripe for the picking. Passing on the aisles where highly packaged and marketed items are stocked, and staying on course around the edges of your supermarket can save you 5% to 20% on your grocery bill. Foods high in nutrition and low on food science and marketing claims bring greater value to your family meals.

BOTTOM LINE: Limiting your exposure to the supermarket aisles and shopping around the edges can save you between $7.50 and $30 on a $150 trip to the grocery store and delivers more nutritional value to your dinner table per dollar spent.

➤ **Stock up with sales and clip online coupons.** Planning ahead by shopping grocery sales and using coupons is good for your health and for your wallet. Saving money on the food you regularly need for weekly meals is the best type of deal. Check your favourite grocery stores' websites to see if they offer online printable coupons to download. You may need to register or become a member on their site to get access to the best deals on whole foods like lean meats, dried beans, dairy, brown rice, fruits and vegetables—but it's worth it. Whole foods present the best savings, since they can be frozen or kept in a pantry for when food prices increase. Stocking up on your grocery basics when they're on sale can save you hundreds every few months and helps you stretch limited food dollars.

BOTTOM LINE: If you save 30 cents on a can of concentrated orange juice and go through three cans each week, you'll save

almost $50 per year just on orange juice. So watch the flyers and check for online coupons to make small reductions that add up to big savings on whole foods and grocery basics.

➤ **Shop strategically in bulk.** To save maximum bucks when hitting the bulk shops, be sure to think strategically before buying that oversized jug of ketchup on sale. If the food spoils before you get to use it up, chances are the deal is a bust. The best way to shop for larger quantities and save on your grocery bill is to buy only those products you need and use frequently, such as a 5 kg jar of peanut butter for family lunches. Buying bigger quantities can also save on packaging when you consider the lesser impact a single 5 kg jar of peanut butter has over five separate 1 kg jars. Another bulk saving strategy is to visit the bulk-bin aisle in your grocery store. Bulk bins are an incredible source of generic pasta, rice, dried beans, tea, spices, sweets and nut butters for up to 60% less than brand-name versions in fancy boxes with colourful marketing. Just fill a bag with the bulk ingredients you need and see your savings add up.

BOTTOM LINE: Cut your food bill by thousands each year by shopping for bulk grocery items strategically and by checking out the foods in the bulk-bin aisle.

➤**Eat less meat.** To save hundreds on groceries, try using less meat in your family meals. You don't have to go vegetarian—simply try some meatless dishes even just once a week by adding alternatives like protein-rich beans to a few dishes. Switching from animal protein to bean protein is a wonderfully frugal way to add some dollars to your bank account and find some variety in your diet. Soak and cook dried beans to become the ultimate money-saving bean counter. For more details see the feature "How to Soak and Cook Dried Beans" in this chapter.

BOTTOM LINE: Eating less meat and more meat alternatives like dried beans bought in bulk can save you hundreds on your grocery bill. For example, enough chicken to feed dinner to a hungry family of four costs around $15, while the beans for an equally filling meal cost under $2. Eating like this once a week saves over $650 a year.

➤ **Brown-bag your lunch.** Taking a homemade lunch to school or work every day could save you thousands a year. It's easy to be tempted to spend money when you're hungry, and there are plenty of restaurants selling convenient meals. But if you eat out for lunch daily at $7 a meal, that adds up to $35 a week, or $1,750 a year. Making your own sandwich or bringing leftovers from dinner costs you less than half and is probably healthier for you.

BOTTOM LINE: Brown-bagging your midday meal can save you $1,125 a year if a homemade meal costs only $2.50.

➤ **Hit the supermarket for a bunch of lunch.** If you're in a pinch and need a frugal midday meal, then hit your local supermarket for the freshest deals. The salad bar is a fantastic place to find an inexpensive leafy lunch—just steer clear of the costly combos and add-ons. Sandwich lovers can rejoice by visiting the deli and bakery aisles. Bulk buns can be had for 30 cents each, and adding some cheese or deli meat to the roll only adds a dollar or two to the deal. At under 50 cents a piece, grabbing a single apple or banana for dessert is a very healthy and cheap way to complete your meal.

BOTTOM LINE: Save big on lunch by putting together your own supermarket sandwich—for under $3.

➤ **Eat dinner at home.** Eating dinner at restaurants or ordering takeout meals costs you big bucks over the course of a year. Eating more meals at home not only puts hundreds of dollars back into your pocket but it leaves you with leftovers for lunch. Making more home-cooked meals is healthier than eating out regularly because you can control portion size, cut sodium levels and lessen fat content. So fatten your wallet by eating at home and you may just slim your waistline while you're at it.

BOTTOM LINE: Ordering a $40 takeout meal just six times a month adds up to $240 per month, or $2,880 per year.

➤ **Make your own coffee.** Like a daily latte with a mocha biscotti on the side? These seemingly small drips of coffee dollars can really add up to a lot of cookie dough when you look at the costs. A daily latte and biscotti can cost $4 daily, or $28 weekly, or $1,456 in a year. To save maximum dollars on your daily coffee break, make your own hot beverage and take homemade biscotti to work.

BOTTOM LINE: Saving almost a thousand dollars a year on taking a break adds up to the equivalent of a free week off work. Now that's my kind of coffee break.

➤ **Leave the liquor.** Spirits are fun, but lots of liquor can leave your pocketbook dry. Try drinking less alcohol to help boost your savings. A bottle of nice red wine costs $15 to $25, and most of the cost is in tax. Drinking two fewer bottles a month or leaving a few bottles of beer on the wall can save you a lot. Alternatively, make your own beer and wine at home, since cutting out the taxman saves you hundreds. You can also search out features on good bottles of wine under $15 in the food section of your local paper.

BOTTOM LINE: Drinking less alcohol each month can save you as much as $50, while brewing your own spirits could save you some tax dollars—and perhaps make you some friends.

➤ **Shop in season.** Buying in-season fruits and vegetables keeps your grocery costs down, so shop at local farmers' markets and freeze perishables like berries and vegetables. Eating frozen local, seasonal blueberries in oatmeal for breakfast is delicious *and* frugal in the winter months. Planning ahead and freezing farmers' market finds saves you from buying more expensive out-of-season produce. See the feature "Freeze Food for Big Savings" in this chapter.

BOTTOM LINE: Buy fruits and vegetables in season and freeze, dehydrate or can them for the winter months to save at least 30%. For example, a pint of strawberries can cost as much as $5.99 in the winter; freeze $2 pints in summer to save a cool $4 per week on berry bliss!

Change Your Fridge Habits and Save

Rethinking how you use your fridge daily could save you $30 annually by consuming less energy. Changing your habits is free and easy to do with these simple tips.

- Cool foods before storing. Foods at room temperature require less energy to cool than warmer perishables.

- Keep the doors shut. An open door leaks cold air and makes your fridge work harder. Don't leave the door open while you're considering what to have for dinner.

- Cover foods with a lid or plastic wrap before storing. Uncovered foods release moisture and force the cooling unit to use more energy.

- Organize your freezer by storing food flat and making the most of your space. A well-organized space allows the cool air to circulate more efficiently.

- Fill unused freezer space with water-filled containers to optimize energy use and to keep your food frozen in the event of a power outage. The ice blocks will keep food cold longer when the power is out and reduce the amount of air that needs to be cooled every time you open the freezer door. ■

➤ **Buy organic pesticide-free foods only when it's worth it.**
Foods touting the "organic" label are quickly taking over
grocery shelves despite their sometimes steep sticker price,
which can easily be double that of conventionally grown
foods. But is paying this added premium to avoid pesticide exposure worth the cost? The answer is both yes and
no. The U.S. Department of Agriculture has found that
even after you wash certain fruits and vegetables, they still
contain much higher levels of pesticide residue than others. If you've got some extra dollars in your budget, you
may consider buying the following 12 foods as organics
because their conventionally grown counterparts tend to
be laden with pesticides.

12 organic foods worth buying to avoid pesticides

Apples	Grapes	Potatoes
Bell peppers	Nectarines	Raspberries
Celery	Peaches	Spinach
Cherries	Pears	Strawberries

12 organic foods not worth buying when trying to avoid pesticides

Asparagus	Cauliflower	Onions
Avocado	Corn	Papaya
Bananas	Kiwi	Peas
Broccoli	Mangoes	Pineapples

**BOTTOM LINE: Paying double for some organic foods may
be worth the added cost because their conventionally grown
counterparts tend to be laden with pesticides even after**

vigorous washing. But stick to conventional for other fruits and veggies if you're looking to keep your budget in line.

➤ **Learn to love leftovers.** Cooking meals while planning for leftovers can save you big dollars throughout the year. Cooking larger meals helps you take advantage of economies of scale; one big batch of food can take less time and cost less to prepare than several smaller meals. Preparing larger portions also saves on energy costs associated with cooking food. Planned leftovers are advantageous for busy families because they can be taken to school or work for lunches, saving on eating out. Cooking on weekends and freezing portion sizes for future meals can cut costs by hundreds a year and save you time. See the feature "Loving Leftovers for Less."
BOTTOM LINE: Learn to love leftovers and make larger meals to save you precious time and money. Preparing two meals' worth of food each time you cook can save up to half of your cooking energy needs.

➤ **Cook with less energy.** Sometimes a smaller cooking appliance can do the job of an energy-hungry oven. Because they consume less electricity, smaller appliances like slow cookers, toaster ovens and microwaves can cook a family meal for a lot less. Use a toaster oven to heat a meal in the same amount of time as an oven and save around $50 per year in energy costs. When boiling water in a kettle, only boil as much as you need. To reduce your cooking energy consumption further, consider adding more raw foods to your diet. Foods like salads, fruits and raw vegetables are good for you and don't require heating.

BOTTOM LINE: Switch off your oven and use smaller appliances to reduce your energy costs by at least $50 a year.

➤ **Sack plastic bags by using reusable bags.** Many grocery stores now charge 2 to 5 cents per plastic shopping bag at the checkout. Spending a few bucks on bags per month may sound like nothing today, but the costs can add up to hundreds over the years. While keeping costs down is a concern for many, there are more pressing plastic matters at stake. Disposable plastic bags litter our environment, contribute to climate change and can harm wildlife. Buying a quality reusable bag made from durable and washable rip-stop nylon (like the BAGGU brand for $8 each, or less if you buy multiples) can help you save money while keeping disposables out of the landfill. Even the 99-cent versions for sale at the supermarket make a great option. Many reusable bags can squish into a small package for easy storage in a purse or pocket when you're on the go.

BOTTOM LINE: Save money and keep plastic out of landfills by investing in quality reusable shopping bags. For example, by not using 10 plastic bags a week, you can save about $26 a year.

Freeze Food for Big Savings

Not long ago I remember watching both my grandmother and mom preserve fruits and vegetables by canning, freezing and dehydrating. Canning can get involved, but freezing foods doesn't take a lot of time and is a fantastic way to preserve meals prepared in advance. I often cook a large lasagne, soup or stew on weekends and freeze portions for meals during the month. Making meals in advance not only saves money but saves time on weeknights after a busy day at work.

Most foods freeze well, with the exception of leafy greens and some produce with a high water content. Stick to freezing fruits and vegetables like apples and tomatoes. Before starting upon a frugal freezing adventure, organize your current frozen food situation by discarding vintage parcels. Knowing what's currently on hand and dating packages saves the cost of buying duplicates and replacing perishable foods.

Chop and freeze. To maximize freezer space, chop awkwardly shaped fruits and vegetables (like bananas, asparagus or kale) into bite-sized pieces before freezing. Cut larger items into handy single-serve portions.

Squeeze the air out. Remove as much air as possible from the freezer bag to save room in the freezer and to prevent freezer burn. Buying a vacuum sealer to remove excess air from freezer bags costs around $50, but using a straw and sucking the air out of the freezer bag is free.

Mark the date and keep track. Before freezing fresh produce, be sure to write the date on each bag or container. Even in a freezer food won't last forever—so to avoid thawing something from the Ice Age, be sure to keep track of what you have and rotate your food frequently. Keeping a list of your freezer contents in the kitchen can also help you plan meals and remember what you have on hand.

Freeze in flat packages. Use freezer bags and reusable containers to freeze food flat and save room in the freezer. Stacking food in an organized manner keeps packages from bursting open and helps you find food fast. If you have store-bought packages that are an awkward fit, take the food out and divide it into smaller containers to save space. ■

➤ **Maintain your refrigerator and freezer.** A well-maintained refrigerator and freezer can save you hundreds of dollars in lost energy costs over the year. To keep your older unit running as efficiently as possible, regularly inspect and clean the refrigerator door seals and heating coils. Door seals, also called gaskets, can deteriorate over time, leaving your fridge leaking cool air and cold cash. Replacement gaskets could cost as little as $30 but require $60 in labour costs. Cleaning the dust from your refrigerator coils twice a year is free and makes it easier for the unit to disperse heat, thus making it more efficient when cooling food. A final tip for maintaining your refrigerator and freezer is to defrost at least twice a year.

BOTTOM LINE: Regular maintenance of your older refrigerator gaskets, coils and frost levels is free and can extend the life of the appliance, saving you hundreds in replacement costs.

➤ **Unplug the second refrigerator or freezer.** Second refrigerators and freezers are often underused appliances and tend to be older, less efficient models. If your second unit is running constantly just to cool a few perishables, then unplug it. Using a larger refrigerator or freezer is more efficient and costs less than running two smaller units.

BOTTOM LINE: Unplugging underused refrigerators is free and can save you over $100 a year.

➤ **Replace older inefficient refrigerators.** Keeping an older refrigerator running in your kitchen can cost you. Compared with newer models, ancient units can use up to double the amount of energy to operate, costing you hundreds in additional dollars a year. Recent improvements in refrigerators, ranging from better compressors to improved insulation, have increased energy efficiency dramatically. Replacing an old fridge with a new model can keep your food cool for less and may pay for itself in a few short years given the dramatic cuts to energy use. If you're in the position to purchase a new model, shop around and find a unit big enough to suit your family's needs. Don't be afraid to take along the products or food containers you often refrigerate. Refrigerators are used differently by everyone, so finding the right-sized door compartments and customizable drawers is essential to keeping your food fresh.

BOTTOM LINE: If your refrigerator or freezer is old or not cooling well, it might be a good idea to replace the unit with an ENERGY STAR appliance. Switching to more energy-efficient appliances can save you hundreds a year in energy costs and may keep your perishables fresher, saving you money on your food bill as well.

➤ **Do fewer dishes.** If you can cut down on the number of dishes you need to wash, you can save on water, energy and soap, and your dish pan hands will thank you. While we all would love fewer dirty dishes in our lives, sometimes they seem unavoidable. One easy method is to reuse drinking glasses by giving each member of your family one glass and labelling it. Another method to cut back on the grease is to plan the meals you cook ahead of time. Using a single pot or pan to prepare a meal, reusing cutlery to stir and mix sauces or serving with fewer dishes and getting your family to help themselves rather than using serving plates can drastically reduce the number of dirty dishes in your kitchen.

BOTTOM LINE: Reusing drinking glasses and planning meals ahead of time saves you money on energy, water and soap— and may just keep your hands happy too.

➤ **Wash dishes by hand the frugal way.** It's hard to think fun and frugal thoughts when you're facing a sink full of dirty dishes. But there are ways to cut the costs on cleaning up after dinner if you wash dishes by hand and have a sense of humour about it. Start by limiting the amount of warm or hot water you use to rinse dishes by filling your second sink with clear hot water for rinsing and using your main sink for soapy washing. If you have only one sink, use a plastic pail or big bowl for rinsing dishes. When tackling your dishes, organizing the order in which you clean them can pay off in energy savings. Save your soapy suds by washing glassware first, then silverware and the cleanest dishes and leaving greasy dishes or pots to the end. This helps keep your water clean longer and your dishes grease free.

BOTTOM LINE: Save up to 10% on your dishwashing energy expenses by rinsing in a second sink and organizing the order in which you wash.

➤ **Open the dishwasher door to air-dry dishes.** Skip your dishwasher's heat drying cycle and save on your total dishwashing energy costs by choosing the air-dry option or by opening the dishwasher door to air-dry dishes after the final rinse.

BOTTOM LINE: Start an open-door policy by air-drying dishes and save at least $20 a year on energy costs.

➤ **Maximize your dishwasher.** Get the most out of your dishwasher with these free quick and dirty techniques to save money on hot water. Before starting a load of dirty dishes, be sure your washer is stacked to the brim. Half loads use the same amount of hot water as a full machine, costing you double to clean the same number of dishes.

Another energy-saving technique is to wash using the light or quick cycles. These shorter cycles can use up to 50% less energy than those longer cleaning options while still washing your dishes clean. A final way to save on dirty dishes while saving dish pan hands is to stop pre-rinsing your dishes in the sink. Most modern machines can handle dinner grime and don't require a pre-rinse—just scrape away larger food pieces and load with less effort.

BOTTOM LINE: By washing only full loads, using energy-saving wash cycles and not pre-rinsing your dishes, it's possible to reduce your dishwashing energy costs by 15%.

Save almost $1,000 per year by skipping and swapping

The price of food and kitchen staples at the supermarket is on the rise. Don't be held a financial food hostage at the checkout—here's how to cut your grocery expenses and still enjoy the foods you love. By skipping heavily marketed and packaged products and swapping them for items not featured in flashy displays, you can save drastically on your food costs. Here's a list of weekly purchases that show how skipping on brand-name products and swapping for inexpensive alternatives can save you nearly $1,000 on groceries each year.

Water

Skip: brand-name bottled water, 6 × 710 mL
    for $3.49 or $0.81/L

Swap: tap water—virtually free!

BOTTOM LINE: Save $3.49. Bottled water can cost as much as gasoline. Switch to tap water to save money while also decreasing your environmental footprint.

Orange Juice

Skip: brand-name frozen concentrate, 1 can for $1.48
    makes 1.4 L, or $1.06/L

Swap: generic frozen concentrate, 1 can for $1.18 makes
    1.4 L, or $0.84/L

Skip: brand-name from concentrate, 1.89 L for $3.87,
    or $2.05/L

Swap: generic from concentrate: 1.89 L for $2.97, or $1.57/L

BOTTOM LINE: Save 90 cents. Buying cans of frozen orange juice concentrate and adding your own water saves you 50% over buying premixed frozen juice from concentrate. The frozen juice can also be stored much longer.

Pasta

Skip: brand-name pasta, 375 g box for $2.99, or $0.80/100 g

Swap: bulk pasta, $0.39/100 g

BOTTOM LINE: Save $1.53. The savings from buying bulk over packaged pasta can be up to 50%.

Rice

Skip: brand-name rice, 500 g box for $4.99, or $0.50/100 g

Swap: bulk white long grain rice, $0.22/100 g

BOTTOM LINE: Save $3.89. Packaged rice can cost up to four times the price of bulk. Save 75% by buying in bulk.

Oatmeal

Skip: brand-name oatmeal, 375 g for $2.89, or $0.77/100 g

Swap: bulk oatmeal, $0.24/100 g

BOTTOM LINE: Save $1.99. Bulk oatmeal is a third the price of oatmeal in pretty packages.

HEALTH BONUS: Oatmeal bought in bulk costs less and doesn't contain all the added sugars, preservatives or spices found in the brand-name single-serving products. If you like your oats flavoured with cinnamon, just add some to your morning breakfast.

Peanut Butter

Skip: brand-name crunchy peanut butter, 1 kg for $8.10,
    or $0.81/100 g

Swap: bulk crunchy peanut butter, 1 kg for $4.90,
    or $0.49/100 g

BOTTOM LINE: Save $3.20. The brand name costs 1.7 times more than bulk. Switching to bulk peanut butter saves you 35%.

HEALTH BONUS: Not only does the bulk peanut butter save you money, it's healthier for you too because it's not hydrogenated like the brand-name.

Lettuce

Skip: brand-name, 1 head (in a 216 g bag) for $3.98

Swap: 1 head of green leafy lettuce, $1.28

BOTTOM LINE: Save $2.70. Prepared lettuce in a bag costs more than twice the price of a whole head of lettuce. Switching to lettuce heads saves you 50% on healthy leafy goodness.

Carrots

Skip: brand-name bagged peeled carrots, $1.68/pound

Swap: bulk carrots, $0.68/pound

BOTTOM LINE: Save $1.00. Switching from bagged peeled carrots to bulk ones sold in the produce aisle saves you 60%. You pay a huge premium of 2.5 times for the marketing and convenience of prepared carrots.

TOTAL WEEKLY SAVINGS: $18.70
TOTAL YEARLY SAVINGS: $972.40 ■

Loving Leftovers for Less

There are three types of leftovers you can prepare to save you big money on your grocery bill: planned-overs, unplanned leftovers and mixed meals. Learning to love leftovers can save you food preparation time and money.

Planned-Overs. A planned-over meal is a fun definition for making enough food for additional meals. By planning ahead when preparing one meal and making extra, you can take advantage of economies of scale; one big batch takes less time to cook and costs less than many smaller meals. You can also save time on preparing future meals and save energy from constantly cooking new recipes. The best planned-overs are meals you can save and freeze for another day or refrigerate for the week. Meals that make incredible planned-overs include lasagne, stews, soups, casseroles, chili and presoaked and cooked beans. Beans are possibly the best ingredient to have on hand in the frugal kitchen because they can be added to most dishes and they blend well with most flavours.

Surprise Leftovers. If you're lucky enough to have a little extra left over after a meal, don't scrape it into the trash and throw it away. Package those leftovers in containers and refrigerate for tomorrow's lunch. Sometimes a meal just tastes better the second time around, and taking a homemade meal to work or school for lunch can save you money because you won't have to eat out. If you've got enough left over for an entire meal, then freeze or refrigerate for use in the future.

It's-a-Mix Meals. Meals combining ingredients from previous dinners require creativity and a sense of adventure. Sometimes the best-tasting meals are those repurposed from another meal or extended by mixing in rice, pasta, vegetables or quinoa or put on flatbread to make pizza. Adding leftover sauces or vegetables to make a casserole is a delicious way to save on your food budget. Mix cold leftovers like chicken into a salad or heat them up with beans and rice. Feed the family on a few dollars by mixing canned tuna or salmon with pasta and vegetables in a casserole. The Internet can be a great tool here—just search for all the ingredients you have on hand and see what turns up. The next time you have a variety of ingredients hanging around your kitchen, stretch your mind and try a mixed meal to save some serious cash. ■

How to Soak and Cook Dried Beans

Soaking and cooking dried beans is a frugal way to get a protein-packed meal filled with heart-healthy nutrients for less than the cost of meat. Beans are delicious in many dishes and are a good source of folic acid, magnesium and fibre. But beware—beans can also give you a healthy dose of gas if they're not prepared correctly. If you don't want to be firing on all cylinders, then I strongly suggest you soak your beans to help break down all the complex sugars, like the indigestible oligosaccharides, to prevent gastrointestinal gusts. If you're the very breezy type, then consider soaking your beans even longer to maximize the amount of sugars dissolved.

Dried and canned bean equivalents. Buying dried beans is extremely cheap. You can get significantly more beans by forgoing the canned variety because dried beans expand when soaked, so you end up with even more beans per dollar.

A pound of dried beans (about 2 cups/500 mL) yields 5 to 6 cups (1.25 to 1.5 L) of cooked beans.

One 19-ounce (540 mL) can of beans yields about 2 cups (500 mL) of cooked beans.

Soaking. There are two methods for soaking dried beans: the long soak and the quick soak. In general, the larger the bean (for example, chickpeas and kidney beans), the longer they need to soak to soften and expand to full size. The long soak method will give you the best results, but if you're in a hurry and don't mind risking a few burst bean skins, then use the quick soak method.

LONG SOAK: Rinse the beans and discard any abnormal-looking ones and debris, then place them in a large bowl with enough cold water to cover them by 2 inches. Let the beans soak for at least 8 hours or overnight. Drain.

QUICK SOAK: Rinse and pick over the beans, then place them in a large pot with enough cold water to cover them by 2 inches. Bring to a boil. Boil for 2 minutes. Cover, remove from the heat and let stand for 1 hour. Drain.

(Some small beans and legumes, like lentils and split peas, cook so quickly that they don't need to be soaked at all.)

Cooking. Cooking soaked beans is easy. If you're going to be around the home, then use the conventional stovetop method. If you're out and about and have hours to let your beans boil, then use the slow cooker method.

STOVETOP: Place the drained soaked beans in a large pot and add enough cold water to cover them by 2 inches. Bring to a boil, skimming off any foam that rises to the surface. Reduce the heat to low and simmer, stirring occasionally, until the beans are tender, about 1 to 2 hours.

SLOW COOKER: Place the drained soaked beans in a slow cooker and pour in 5 cups (1.25 L) of boiling water. Cover and cook on high until tender, about 2 to 4 hours. ■

CHAPTER 9

Living Room and Dining Room

Living and dining rooms were once rarely used places, set aside for formal social occasions. They were where we kept our most expensive furniture and ate from our fine china. Today, modern homes and modern lifestyles have turned living and dining rooms into dens, family rooms and eat-in kitchens, but no matter what you call them, the spaces where you entertain your family and friends can be expensive. Between furnishing them in a functional and appealing way that makes you proud to open them to guests, and just keeping yourself cozy and entertained, there are lots of ways to save in your living and dining room—you simply need to be creative and learn from what you see around you (because entertaining and decorating are the best areas to borrow thrifty ideas from other people).

Years ago when I bought my first sofa, it was a wingback four-seater covered in bright blue microfibre fabric. In the store, the big blue sofa seemed like a fun and brilliant idea, but getting it home was anything but fun. I hadn't done my homework and nearly had to send the sofa back because it wouldn't even fit through my front door. Within months I felt overwhelmed by the piece and how the blue luminescence dominated the space, limiting my ability to change the look of my living room. A neutral-coloured sofa in beige, brown or white would have given me greater flexibility in decorating options and lasted for years.

Whenever I think of entertaining and decorating, I always think back to the big blue sofa because I learned so much from it: that planning for the long term is better than impulse-buying a single, high-impact piece; you have to do your homework to make sure something is going to fit in your space (both physically and decor-wise); you have to be able to think creatively to work with what you've got (no matter how big and blue it might be); and in the end, entertaining isn't about the glamour or hue of your sofa. Now I think back fondly of my sofa because of all of the great parties it hosted, the visits with friends it accommodated and the times it gave beloved guests (well, and me!) a place to crash. Entertaining is all about keeping people happy, which makes it easy to do on a dime. Here are some of my best suggestions for fun, frugal decorating and entertaining.

Furniture and Decorating

➤ **Go shopping in your basement.** The next time you need a fresh look for your living room or a setting for your dining room table, take a tip from the design blog Apartment Therapy (apartmenttherapy.com) and go shopping in your own home. If you look around before hitting the shops, chances are that all the things you need to entertain for less are already just sitting in closets or hiding on shelves around your home. Ideas include raiding your bedroom closet to convert clothing you no longer wear into fabric for throw pillows; finding family antiques like fine china, teacups or silverware and using them to serve guests; or just picking some flowers from your garden and turning them into a table setting. The possibilities of what you can do with the stuff you already own are endless and could save you from spending on decorations and other things you don't need.

BOTTOM LINE: Save hundreds of dollars by going on a shopping spree in your closets and attic, and finding new decorative uses for forgotten treasures.

➤ **Buy mis-tinted paint for smaller surfaces.** Buying a quart of paint to change up a wall or put a fresh coat on an old table can be costly—about $15. To save some bucks on painting, check out the mis-tint or pre-tinted paints section in your hardware or paint store. They are often very good quality at a greatly reduced price and may be the perfect shade for your project. You may even find a bigger batch of mistakenly tinted paints and have enough to paint an entire room!

BOTTOM LINE: Save 30% to 50% by choosing a pre-tinted or mis-tinted paint the next time you're looking to freshen a surface.

➤ **Keep things neutral.** Black, white and beige may sound terribly boring, but selecting a neutral colour palette on furniture throughout your home could save you thousands over the years. When decorating your rooms, invest in quality neutral pieces like side tables, bookcases, chairs and sofas so that you'll be able to easily and inexpensively reinvent your décor in the years to come. A beige sofa with white side tables can be accessorized with colourful throw pillows, bright artwork and a fun centrepiece to change things up for less. You could get 10 different looks with a single neutral sofa just by changing the shade of your walls.

BOTTOM LINE: Think long term and save thousands—buy neutral furnishings that stand the test of time and quality pieces that last for generations. A big blue sofa may sound like a fun buy today but will end up costing you hundreds when you tire of the shade and need a new seat.

➤ **Negative space can be a positive.** You don't need to fill every square inch in your home with stuff to make it look great. Sometimes less is more—and buying fewer things saves a lot of money. Make decisions about furniture, art and decorations based on value rather than quantity, and keep some airy space in each room to evoke a feeling of calm rather than clutter. As a bonus, you'll have more floor space to stretch out on or play with your kids. If you've already got too much stuff, check out "Selling Tactics" in Chapter 4 and turn some of that clutter into cash.

BOTTOM LINE: Filling every corner with furniture can be expensive, costing you thousands of extra dollars. Say yes to less and your wallet will thank you.

➤ **Measure twice and buy once.** Before bringing home that harvest dining table or big comfy sofa, make sure the furniture you want to buy is going to fit your space. Try using old cardboard boxes and painter's tape to see how certain furniture sizes will function and look. Painter's tape is an inexpensive and valuable tool for marking rug and sofa dimensions in a room and can save you from spending good money on poorly planned furnishings. Make sure that you also carefully measure door frames, elevators, hallways and staircases so you're not stuck with a big blue sofa sticking out your front door when the delivery truck leaves. Many retailers will take a sofa back if you can't fit it in but may charge you a costly restocking fee.

BOTTOM LINE: Stay in the right dimension by measuring and planning your space before you buy big pieces of furniture. Planning ahead and measuring with painter's tape costs only $3 and can save thousands of dollars and hours of frustration.

➤ **Move furniture around.** Every so often we all need a change. But buying new furniture for your living or dining rooms is expensive, so before breaking the bank why not try moving stuff around your home and see how things look? Try putting your sofa against another wall, moving your bookshelves from the office to the living room or changing the angle of your dining room table. And don't be afraid to try old pieces in totally new functions—maybe a bedside table would be perfect in your entryway, or a grouping of side tables could make a brand-new coffee table. Often all that's needed to freshen and revive a living space is a little change using the furniture you already own.

BOTTOM LINE: Pulling your furniture away from the walls, positioning things on a new angle and changing up the way you're using old pieces can bring excitement to a previously tired arrangement for absolutely no money at all.

➤ **Skip the sofa bed.** A sofa that can function as a bed for guests may seem like a great thrifty idea, but think again. Sofa beds cost hundreds more than an equivalent sofa, are heavy and hard to move and often force guests to sleep in your living room. Skip the sofa bed and save hundreds by getting an inflatable "bed in a box" kit that can be inflated in any room of the house and then stored away out of sight. Inflatable beds are easy to move, are just as comfortable as sofa beds (maybe even more so) and add up to considerable savings.

BOTTOM LINE: Save hundreds by getting a regular sofa of good quality and buy an inflatable "bed in a box" for when guests stay the night.

➤ **Buy a sofa with a good frame.** Sofas with a good-quality kiln-dried hardwood frame can last decades, with many manufacturers offering 25-year guarantees on their better furniture frames. In comparison, cheaper frames made from particleboard, staples and softwood can eventually warp or even crack from weight or moisture. Both frame types can be re-upholstered with new foam cushioning and new fabric, but a warped or damaged frame generally cannot be repaired. Be sure to ask salespeople about the sofa's frame construction before buying so you know what you're getting on the inside.

BOTTOM LINE: Quality kiln-dried hardwood sofa frames generally cost hundreds to thousands more than lesser quality frames. But if you want to love your sofa for years, then invest in a quality construction and save in the longer term.

➤ **Get a sofa with integrated slipcovers.** Not all slipcovers make your sofa look like a loose billowy marshmallow. Many sofas come with removable covers that fit snugly around the cushions, arms and backing, making the piece look seamless. A slipcover can be easily washed and cleaned when the inevitable happens—something spills from a juice cup or a pet makes its mark—meaning that a minor mishap doesn't require a big financial fix. From a décor point of view, owning a few slipcovers makes it easy to try fun colours for a season or holiday and then switch back to a calmer shade for the rest of the year. Buying a sofa with a removable cover also allows you to take advantage of the full life of a good-quality frame, because you can just add a new cover when the old one shows wear and tear for far less than the price of re-upholstering.

BOTTOM LINE: Re-upholstering an average-sized sofa costs around $1,000 to $1,500, depending on the fabric you use,

which can be a great savings over replacing a couch entirely. New covers for a sofa with integrated slipcovers—such as Ikea's Stockholm line—cost around $500 to $700 each, saving you up to 50% on the cost of reupholstering. If you own an older Ikea sofa, check out the website bemz.com. They specialize in both cool and neutral slipcover designs for most Ikea furniture starting at about $100, a potential savings of about $900.

Set Up Your Home Office for Less

Not too long ago I set up a modest home office in the corner of a spare bedroom. While sorting bills and writing emails on my sofa had been fun, it was time to get serious and start working from a single, organized location. And I'm not alone in my need for a home office for less. Many households are looking to accommodate a telecommuter, run a small business or just find a central spot for a home computer. A fledgling home office doesn't have to be expensive if you know what items are worth spending bucks on and which items can be bought for less.

Cabinets and Storage. Nothing dooms a home business like cluttered client lists, messy paper piles and unorganized customer orders. Start your start-up right with good storage to keep your paperwork filed and organized—because being organized is critical to staying sane.

Office filing systems can be expensive, but they don't need to be. You can find a commercial-grade set-up with steel cabinets, industrial shelving and sturdy construction for less by looking for local businesses that are moving shop or shutting down. Downsizing companies will often sell nearly-new shelving and filing cabinets dirt cheap. Some stores specialize in used office gear, but be careful, as these consignment shops take a cut for the convenience.

I didn't require heavy-duty gear for my own little home operation, so I decided to go Swedish and shop at Ikea. The best place to shop at Ikea is not upstairs with the installations but downstairs in the hidden-away "as is" section of damaged and discontinued goods. By hunting through the torn boxes, I found several shelving units for 50% off the regular price. My storage unit was in pristine condition but was marked down because the packaging was mangled.

Seating. Spend the money and buy a quality chair. There's no sense being miserable sitting at your desk in a cheap, uncomfortable chair with few adjustable components. Putting the money into a chair with removable arms and adjustable lumbar support, seat height and seat tilt will pay dividends in the quality of work you produce and your personal comfort. Many of my colleagues swear by the ultra-expensive Herman Miller chairs for $1,000 each, but I think this is overkill. There are many reasonably priced chairs with quality components on the market for around $250. The key to buying an office chair is to try it before bringing it home, so don't be shy at the store and do ask to sit in it for a while. Be sure to buy only from stores with a good return policy, in case you need to return your chair because of comfort issues. Your back and buns might just thank you for spending the extra dollars.

Desks. Height is the most important consideration when buying a desk. With repetitive strain injuries being common among computing types, you've got to work at a table height that is healthy for your body. Check out the Canadian Centre for Occupational Health and Safety website (ccohs.ca) for desk-height guidelines. If you find a great deal that isn't the right height, consider options like propping up a desk or trimming the legs.

I bought my simple desk used through a seller I found on Kijiji.ca and saved 80% over buying new. Because I bought my chair and desk separately, I brought my chair to try with the desk to make sure they worked together. Saving money on these items is nice, but buying something uncomfortable is a waste of money. It's only a deal if it works for your body.

When buying a desk, try to avoid ones boasting extra features like integrated cable management systems, storage and CPU holders. All these costly gimmicks can be replaced with DIY solutions.

Computer. Shopping for a new computer can be a daunting task, and your most frugal bet might be to avoid the experience altogether. For most office tasks, the computer you already have might be more than enough. If it's running slowly, just add some extra memory to speed it up. By upgrading my memory for $100, I was able to keep my current machine and save thousands.

But if your computer is circa 1980, then it's probably time to get a new one. But do your research and know what features you need before hitting the shops. Try to avoid stores with commissioned salespeople because they have an interest in selling you more machine than you need. If you can, bring a computer-savvy friend along to help you navigate the price points and weigh the hardware and software options to best suit your needs. If you're not careful, it's easy to spend a small fortune and still end up with little to show for it. Unless you are computing to track and calculate the orbits of hundreds of satellites, take a pass on the latest and greatest technology. I bought my computer for much less by buying a refurbished model a few years ago. She's still running strong, and I saved 30% by getting a previously returned model with a torn box. Just be sure to get a full manufacturer's warranty when buying refurbished electronics.

Free Software. Most computers these days come bundled with one office package or another. If your computer doesn't have office applications or you're looking to upgrade to a newer package, check out the free alternatives. My favourite is a free application called Open Office which can be downloaded from openoffice.org and used completely free of charge for any purpose. Open Office is an open-source software package for word processing, spreadsheets, presentations, graphics, databases and more. Open Office looks like and functions very much like Microsoft Office.

If you have a fast Internet connection and like having the ability to access your documents from anywhere, Google Documents (docs.google.com) offers a free online word processor and spreadsheet application; you will need to create a user account. Google Documents is not as feature-rich as other office applications, but it works quite well. Be aware that all your documents will be stored on Google's servers, so be wary if you have sensitive or confidential information.

Monitor. A good computer monitor is an office essential and worth spending some extra money on. Flat-panel LCD monitors have recently dropped significantly in price, and you can now find a 22-inch LCD monitor for around $300. Keep in mind that "features" like integrated speakers and extra connections will add to the price without improving image quality. Also watch out for higher-end monitors that require expensive video card upgrades on your computer. My advice is to wait for a big sale and then buy from a store with a good no-questions-asked return policy in case the image quality or screen size don't work out for you. Take a pass on the extended warranty to save some extra dollars.

Keyboard and Mouse. Do you really need a wireless Bluetooth keyboard with wild and wonky buttons? How about a wireless laser mouse that scrolls in fifteen different ways? I didn't think so. Pass on the cheesy features and get a mouse and keyboard that won't trap you into paying more. If you're into split ergonomic keyboards, then by all means get one, but they cost more, around $70 each. For most people a simple keyboard for $25 and standard mouse for $10 can get the job done for less.

Printers. Don't get inked by falling for the budget $50 printer only to find that replacement ink or toner cartridges cost $60 every few months. I gave up on printers years ago once the price of ink exceeded the price of the printer. If you don't need to print a lot, then skip buying a printer and save yourself $150 to $400. Instead, share documents through email without printing on a single sheet of paper. When I do need to print, I save the file on an inexpensive USB thumb drive and head to the local copy shop where copies cost pennies a page. A basic 4 GB USB thumb drive costs just $10 and is handy for backing up and carrying your documents wherever you go. If you need to print from home, then look for a basic black-and-white laser printer on sale for about $150 and skip the fancy colour models that start at $250 and require expensive toner replacements. ■

Entertainment

➤ **Break out the board games and host a game night.** Don't roll your eyeballs at the thought of busting out the cardboard and playing a board game. Getting together with a group of friends over drinks and a favourite game is a great way to spend an evening socializing. Sure, there are plenty of classics like Scrabble and Monopoly to choose from, but there are lots of modern choices too. Games like Taboo!, Cranium, Apples to Apples and Pictionary are great for laughing out loud with your friends. If you're more into strategy, try Settlers of Catan, Blokus, Carcassonne, Ticket to Ride, or Trivial Pursuit for a more analytical challenge.

BOTTOM LINE: Board games range from $1 at garage sales to around $100 for new games with more pieces. But once you buy a game, it can provide hours of free entertainment with your family and friends—at less than the cost of a dinner out for two.

➤ **Throw a potluck.** To have more fun and spend less money while entertaining at home, throw a potluck and invite your friends and family to share their favourite dish. Potluck gatherings allow your guests to show off their culinary skills while giving you a break on food preparation and entertaining costs. Just be sure to decide beforehand who brings what or else you may have seven chocolate desserts and no main courses to feast upon. Give the gathering a theme to bring out more creativity in the dishes people bring.

BOTTOM LINE: Throw a potluck lunch or dinner and entertain for the price of a single meal.

➤ **Stream music or TV from the Internet.** Set the soundtrack for your next party for less by streaming free tunes from Internet radio stations. There are thousands of free stations online, and all you need is a high-speed Internet connection to get into the groove. Discover a new channel or find an old favourite by checking out the free listings at shoutcast.com and live365.com and then blast the tunes to your heart's content. These sites list both Internet-only stations and online feeds for commercial radio stations. If you have basic cable or basic satellite, your package may come with commercial-free radio at no extra cost. If you're looking for an alternative to cable TV, most major networks stream some of their programming online and commercial free—so check out cbc.ca/video/ and shows.ctv.ca/video/ to get up-to-date with your favourites online.

BOTTOM LINE: A high-speed Internet connection is all you need to stream music and television for free.

➤ **Download podcasts for free.** Who needs satellite radio or expensive specialty TV programs when you can get free entertainment from podcasts! A podcast is a digital audio or video file you download over the Internet and play back through an iPod, MP3 player or computer. Podcasts range widely in topic, from music shows, audio books and cooking programs to fitness workouts, parenting advice and financial programming. Some podcasts are professionally produced while others are created by everyday people with a passion for a certain topic. To find a topic that interests you, surf on over to iTunes.com and download Apple's iTunes program—it's free! Then search iTunes by entering "podcast" and your favourite terms and see what is available. For example, searches for "triathlon podcast" and "cooking podcast" resulted in two weekly podcast shows I've been listening to for several months.

BOTTOM LINE: Podcasts are free and can provide you with hours of informative entertainment.

➤ **Reduce magazine subscriptions costs.** A yearly subscription could be costing you if the glossy magazines are rarely read. It's possible to fall out of love with a particular topic or periodical over the years but just keep paying renewal rates out of habit. If you're not getting the most from your magazine or newspaper subscriptions, then consider cancelling the service—or split the cost with a friend to save 50%. If you like reading a variety of magazines, then head on over to the library to read dozens of them for free. If you're an impulse buyer and regularly splurge on a certain magazine at the checkout, then get a subscription and cut the newsstand costs by up to 60%.

BOTTOM LINE: Cut your magazine or newspaper subscription costs by at least $25 by cancelling the service, sharing with a friend or reading them at the library.

➤ **Watch for free books online.** There are many opportunities to find the full-length versions of books online. Many publishers make deals with magazines and talk shows to distribute online editions gratis for a set amount of time for those lucky viewers who caught the show. If you catch one of these shows, download your copy and enjoy a new topic or author for free. Search the Net and you may even find an online edition promoted on a blog or a partner website.

BOTTOM LINE: Download free books online during special promotions in magazines, on talk shows or through blogs.

➤ **Love the library.** Save yourself on book bills, DVD rentals, kids' entertainment and music purchases by going to your local library and signing out stuff for free. The library offers more than just books—so bring the whole family and make a big trip out of stocking up on entertainment for less. You might just find a new favourite author, an exciting topic to explore or free music to help you unwind. Be sure to watch out for due dates and fines—these little charges can add up to big dollars fast if you forget to return materials on time!

BOTTOM LINE: Get more bang for your entertainment buck by borrowing books, movies, music and children's materials for free at the library.

➤ **Downgrade your television programming.** If you sub-scribe to all those fancy-dancy cable packages, take a minute to tally how many channels you actually watch. You may be surprised how few stations you regularly tune in to. Keep a journal to track your viewing habits and cancel the pack-ages you don't use. Chances are the majority of programs you watch are on your provider's basic package.
BOTTOM LINE: By downgrading to basic cable or satellite, you can save around $20 each month.

➤ **Negotiate a reduction in package price.** They say eve-rything is negotiable, except death and taxes. So get on the phone and ask your provider to reduce the monthly cost of your television package. Some clever negotiation may be needed on your part, but if you explain that you may cancel because of the cost of service, then often a rate cut will be offered. Always research any introductory offers from competitors beforehand so you can tell your provider there are better deals to be had.
BOTTOM LINE: Save up to 50% on your TV programming by negotiating with your service provider for a decrease in your monthly fee.

➤ **Cut the cable.** The monthly cost of cable or satellite television can add up to a huge expense each year. By getting rid of your TV package you save not only on monthly fees but also on energy consumption. Disconnecting the television also gives you the opportunity to reconnect with family and friends in a social way away from the tube.

BOTTOM LINE: Cutting your cable or satellite subscription can save you $40 to $100 each month or $480 to $1,200 each year.

➤ **Watch local programming for free.** Getting rid of your cable or satellite completely will save you hundreds, but if you still want to catch the occasional show, then hook up a set of rabbit ears and watch local programming for free. Cities boast the best local selection, but rural areas have a few channels available too. If you're sold on antennas, be aware that all Canadian stations are switching from analog to digital signals in 2011, which could render your free setup obsolete. To keep watching you may need to either upgrade your television or purchase a digital converter unit.

BOTTOM LINE: Watching local programming is free and can save you up to $1,000 over a cable or satellite subscription each year.

➤ **Buy a smaller television.** If you're in the market for a brand-new television, consider buying a smaller set. Getting the next sized model up can cost you hundreds of extra dollars just for a little bit more screen. Larger televisions also cost more to operate in electricity use.

BOTTOM LINE: Buying a 32-inch TV instead of a 42-inch set can save you $400—enough for almost a year's worth of basic cable.

Make Your Own Sangria

Sangria is a fun and frugal beverage made with an inexpensive bottle of red wine and the fruit you have on hand. It's fun to drink and easy to serve. And the best part is that there's no need to buy expensive wine to make sangria—just grab a pitcher, chop some fruit and pop a cork. The total cost of sangria varies depending on your choice of ingredients. The super-thrifty ingredients can cost from $11 to $18 for 3 quarts (3 L). This recipe makes about 3 quarts and serves four to six guests, depending on their thirst.

Ingredients
1 orange
1 lemon
1 bottle (750 mL) red wine, whatever fits your budget (this is a great way to use up a cheaper bottle)
1/2 cup (125 mL) brandy or rum (optional but recommended)
2 tablespoons (25 mL) sugar
Other tart (acidic) fruit you have on hand (apples, grapes, kiwis, peaches, etc.)
4 cups (1 L) club soda or ginger ale
Ice

Instructions
- Cut orange and lemon into wedges.
- Squeeze orange and lemon wedges into pitcher and then toss them in. Mix in wine, brandy and sugar, stirring to dissolve sugar. Stir in remaining fruit.
- Refrigerate for 12 to 24 hours.
- Add club soda and ice and serve! ■

CHAPTER 10

Bedroom

You spend a lot of your life sleeping. If you're lucky enough to get eight hours of rest each night, you'll spend a full third of your life in bed! Since we literally sleep for years throughout our lives, it only makes sense to be comfortable in the bedroom.

When it comes to nighttime slumber most of us would pay a bit extra for a quality sleep. But does it make sense to spend thousands, or are there ways to save money? While a comfortable bedroom makes for a good night's sleep, it's not necessary to pay a fortune for reasonable rest. Even if you're a princess who needs the softest mattress, comfort can be found without spending a king's ransom. Savings can be found all throughout the bedroom, from the mattress to the clothing in your closet.

Beds and Bedding

There's nothing like jumping into bed on a quality mattress with fresh sheets. But before drifting off to sleepyland counting sheep on an expensive big-brand mattress, learn how to count your savings by finding the perfect bed and linen set for less. There are countless ways to save on beds and bedding without staying awake late at night worrying about costs.

➤ **Don't get the top model mattress.** Top-end mattresses offer luxury features such as extra pillow tops and higher-quality piping on the edges. The internal construction of these luxury models is often similar to mid-priced ones, and the attached pillow tops can wear out quickly. Save some money by getting a mid-range mattress and a separate good-quality mattress pad. This combination will cost you hundreds less, and you can easily clean or replace the mattress pad as needed.

BOTTOM LINE: Top-end mattresses selling for top dollar may contain the same internal construction as mid-priced models, so opt for the less expensive mattress and buy yourself a quality mattress pad to save hundreds.

➤ **Buy a mismatched mattress set.** Save hundreds by getting a mismatched box spring and mattress set. Every year bedding stores have sales offering deals on their odds and ends where the fabric on the mattresses and box springs doesn't match or has a varying pattern.

BOTTOM LINE: Get a great night's sleep by spending up to 50% less on a mismatched mattress set. Once the bedding is tucked around your mattress, you won't see colour and pattern variations anyway.

➤ **Or skip the box spring and get a slatted bed.** Save a few hundred dollars when buying a new mattress by getting a slatted bed and saying goodbye to the box spring. In a slatted bed, the mattress is supported by wooden slats in the bed frame. The advantages of a slatted bed are many: they provide more ventilation to the mattress, they can increase mattress lifespan by reducing moisture buildup, and you save hundreds by not having to buy a box spring.

BOTTOM LINE: A slatted bed has a longer lifespan than a box spring mattress due to ventilation and construction. Choosing a slatted bed will save you from replacing a box spring in around 10 years, saving you hundreds.

➤ **Buy a bed based on comfort, not brand name.** Most major manufacturers in North America buy mattress springs from the same company, Leggett & Platt. Because mattress springs boast very similar qualities, try to ignore the marketing flash and base your bed-buying decision on comfort, firmness, lumbar support and cost. Mattresses soften a bit over time, so consider buying one slightly firmer to allow for give.

BOTTOM LINE: Save hundreds of dollars, maybe even a thousand, by ignoring flashy bed marketing and opting for the most comfortable sleep with the best price.

➤ **Don't buy bed linen based on thread count.** Expensive bed linens boasting high thread counts don't necessarily guarantee the best night's sleep. Thread count is the number of threads per square inch in the fabric and does not account for the type or blend of cotton used. Most bed linen thread counts range from 80 to 340, with the ultra-expensive linens being in the 1,200 range. As thread count increases, the yarns in the fabric become thinner and the price increases, while sheets with a lower thread count tend to be made with thicker yarns and cost less. Generally, most sleepyheads are comfortable with a count between 180 and 250. To find the best buys, watch for white sales in the winter months.

BOTTOM LINE: Select linens based on feel, and go with your senses for comfort and softness. Choosing bed linens with a 240-thread count will save you hundreds over a 600-count sheet without sacrificing comfort or durability.

Closets

The stuff stored in your closet can easily add up to thousands of dollars spent on clothing. To prevent a wardrobe malfunction and losing your shirt to poorly stored items, try these tips to keep your clothing mended and mould free.

➤ **Take inventory of the clothing you own.** Knowing what clothing you own packed tight on hangers or tucked away on shelves can help you determine what you need to buy, sell or mend. Spending money on a pair of black pants, even if they're on sale, is wasteful if you already own five pairs packed away from last season. Going through your closet and trying on pants, jackets and sweaters to see what still fits and what looks good with your wardrobe can help bring pieces back into your weekly rotation and save you from buying unnecessary items.

BOTTOM LINE: Take inventory of the clothing you own and the outfits that can be put together to save yourself hundreds on repeat or unnecessary purchases. You may just discover a lost clothing treasure!

➤ **Remove clothing clutter.** Do you still own leg warmers from the 1980s? Perhaps it's time to clean the clutter from your closet and make way for the current decade. Excess clutter can be sold to consignment stores and turn you a small profit while clearing your space for the clothing you currently wear. Who knows, maybe you'll find your next Halloween costume for free!

BOTTOM LINE: Sell your go-go boots and shirts with shoulder pads for a tiny profit or donate your old wardrobe to charities. Keeping your closet clutter free saves your closet space for the items you actually use.

➤ **Use proper cleaning and storage techniques.** Taking care of the clothing you own helps it to last longer. By investing in quality hangers and clothes covers, you can protect your garments from dust, moisture and pests like moths. Clothing made from natural fibres needs plenty of air circulation to keep fabrics from harbouring bugs and mildew, so use quality wood hangers over cheap wire alternatives to keep garments from slouching and packing tight in your closet. Properly folding and stacking sweaters and shirts can also keep your wardrobe lasting longer. A messy pile of shirts on the floor can become damaged or soiled from being trampled upon. A neatly folded stack of tops can be easily accessed and stays wrinkle free for daily wear.

BOTTOM LINE: Use quality wooden hangers at 75 cents each and clothes covers for 85 cents each to protect your clothing from dust, mildew and pests and help it last longer.

➤ **Mend or repair quality clothing.** If you've lost a button or frayed a hem, pick up a sewing kit for $5 and learn how to repair the light damage. Mending and taking care of your jackets, suits, pants and sweaters will keep them fit for years and save you from replacing garments frequently. If you need an older suit taken in or some pants let out, take them to a seamstress or tailor to keep your clothing wearable for less. Getting a suit altered is far less expensive than buying a new one.

BOTTOM LINE: Regular care and maintenance of your wardrobe keeps it wearable for longer. Getting quality items altered by a professional costs less than replacing ill-fitting items.

➤ **Get your shoes resoled.** You've got to have sole! Instead of tossing out shoes with worn heels or soles, get them resoled for the fraction of the price of a new pair. When shoes wear out, it's usually only the sole that's worn—the upper of a shoe, especially on more expensive leather shoes, can outlast the sole many times over. A decent pair of shoes can be resoled about three times before the upper is worn out. Not only will your shoes last much longer, but by rebuilding them you won't have to put up with the discomfort of breaking in a brand-new pair. Not all shoes—such as running shoes—can be resoled, but you may be surprised with the handy techniques a cobbler can use to save your sole.

BOTTOM LINE: If you resole a $200 pair of shoes three times for $50, you'll spend a total of $350. That saves you $450 over buying a new pair of shoes each time.

➤ **Invest in quality clothing essentials.** Most every guy and gal needs some classic essential pieces in their wardrobe. If you spend a little more on quality fabrics with more durable construction, the basic components of your wardrobe will last for many seasons rather than fall apart after a few months of wear. Keeping essential pieces in your wardrobe longer keeps you from spending hundreds of extra dollars on replacement items.

For gals, look to spend a little extra on the following wardrobe basics:

Pair of dark denim jeans

Dark skirt

Pair of black dress pants

Little black dress

Classic white shirt

Fine-knit sweater

Jacket or suit blazer

Trench coat

Pair of black heels

Guys should spend the bucks and invest in these wardrobe basics:

Dark denim jeans

Sharp-looking suit

Good shirts—classic white and
various colours or patterns

Fine-knit sweater

Tie

Pair of dress pants

Pair of black shoes

BOTTOM LINE: Spend about 15% to 20% more on wardrobe basics or classic pieces and save money in the long run by keeping quality garments longer.

➤ **Buy trendy clothing at discount stores.** Keeping up with trends and looking up-to-date is fun, and important when you work in an office or are around customers. The problem with trends is they usually don't last past a season or two. So save some money by adding trendy pieces to your wardrobe sparingly and shopping for sales at stores like Winners, Joe Fresh and warehouse outlets. You don't need to buy the highest-quality pieces for short-living trends, so save your bigger wardrobe dollars for your clothing essentials, like a quality pea coat or little black dress.

BOTTOM LINE: Have some fun with your wardrobe by adding trendy pieces found on sale or through discount stores and save up to 50%.

➤ **Store your jewellery with care.** Don't get your neck-laces tied in a knot! Lumping your gold and silver chains into a single pile can cause them to tangle into a mass of mess. Trying to pry your favourite chain apart can weaken the links, shortening its lifespan. When storing fine chains, lay them flat in a box to keep them untangled. When storing delicate gems like pearls and amber, place them in a soft cloth bag or pouch or wrap in a soft non-abrasive cloth. With delicate gems, care must be taken to store them safely because their softness makes them more susceptible to damage. Keep soft stones far from sharp objects that may cause scratches; never store them near harsh chemicals like perfumes, which can cause discoloration; and never expose delicate gems to high heat. Lastly, pearls should be kept in a container with lots of ventilation.

BOTTOM LINE: Storing your chains and delicate jewellery carefully means you won't have to repair or replace them— saving you thousands.

How to Clean a Diamond Ring

Avoid spending $70 on expensive ultrasonic jewellery cleaners or time-consuming visits to your jeweller by trying this safe and frugal trick for cleaning your diamond ring. This method works well on yellow gold, white gold and platinum shanks.

What You Need
- 70% isopropyl rubbing alcohol for $1.75 from a drugstore
- Soft eye makeup brush for 99 cents from a drugstore
- Facial tissue for 1 cent

Instructions

1. Place your ring in a small dish filled with enough rubbing alcohol to cover the diamond. (Instead of rubbing alcohol you can use one drop of liquid dish detergent and very hot water.)
2. Soak the ring for 2 minutes.
3. Brush the ring carefully yet vigorously with a soft brush. Be sure to scrub between setting prongs and under the basket and shank.
4. Soak the ring again for at least 2 minutes, and then dry on a tissue. Your diamond ring will look brand new.
5. Repeat every other day for sparkling results. ■

CHAPTER 11

Kids' Rooms and Beyond

As a parent, you never want to feel like you're scrimping where your kids are concerned. Childhood goes by so quickly, and the memories last forever, so many moms and dads find themselves opting into everything, trying to give their kids the best experience possible. But once you've been to your third birthday party in a row and then get hit up for hockey/ballet/piano fee number four for the month, things can get expensive. Yet there are tons of simple, commonsense ways to cut back on outgoing cash without cutting back on the quality of your kids' experience. Whether you're shopping for clothes or eating out, a little creativity and a keen eye for the bottom line can make a huge impact on your family spending. And teaching your kids right from the start that frugal living can be fun is a great way to help them adopt thrifty habits for life. Here are some easy ideas for ways to make a happy childhood more wallet friendly.

➤ **Cut back on baby stuff.** First-time parents can get caught up in the excitement and buy carloads of unnecessary baby items. Talk to friends who have recently had babies and get the lowdown on what's really useful and what's just expensive clutter. Many parents find they don't need a bassinet (babies outgrow them so quickly) or change table (a towel on the bed or even on the floor works just as well). Those disposal systems that wrap the diapers in plastic are not only a waste of money but an environmental nuisance as well.
BOTTOM LINE: Say no to the Diaper Genie and save $35 off the top, plus $8 for every refill pack.

➤ **Buy large items second-hand—but be careful.** Strollers, cribs and car seats are among the most expensive necessities for parents of babies. You can save big by inheriting these items from family or friends, or by buying them second-hand from a consignment shop. Just be aware of the safety issues: for example, if you use a second-hand crib, make sure it's in good condition and includes the label with model number and date of manufacture (so you can check for recalls), and always invest in a new mattress. Buying a used car seat from someone you don't know is not a good idea, as it may have been in an accident. Any second-hand car seat should include the manual so you know exactly how to install and use it.
BOTTOM LINE: New cribs go for $300 and up, sturdy strollers start around $120, and convertible car seats can be well over $200. You should be able to pick up second-hand items for no more than half their original cost—a savings of at least $300.

➤ **Consider cloth diapers.** Your choice of diapers depends entirely on your yuck factor, but cloth diapers will certainly save money compared to disposables. Don't let your mother talk you out of trying them: they're much more absorbent and tight-fitting than they once were. If you're committed to disposables, try the generic brands (they're about 30% cheaper), at least part-time. Many parents find they're not as absorbent, but they should do the trick when you're at home during the day. Save the more expensive brand-name diapers for nighttime and outings.

BOTTOM LINE: Using cloth—even including the expense of rubber pants and laundering—can save you about $1,000 over the 30 months that most kids are in diapers.

➤ **Breastfeed as long as you can.** The decision whether to breastfeed or use a bottle is almost never driven by money, but the cost of formula isn't trivial. If you're committed to nursing but are having a hard time, lots of free support is available from organizations such as La Leche League (lllc.ca). Breastfeeding moms can also save by nixing the disposable breast pads and using washable ones instead.

BOTTOM LINE: Full-time formula users can expect to spend about $100 to $120 a month—a whopping $1,200 a year you can save by breastfeeding.

➤ **Make your own baby food.** You hardly need to be Jamie Oliver to make baby food: all you need is a blender and a freezer. Babies love puréed carrots, sweet potatoes, bananas and pears. You'll save time by making large batches and freezing individual portions in an ice-cube tray—no jars to buy or wash, and you can pop out a portion and thaw as needed. You can even make baby cereals from ground-up rice or from rolled oats. Talk to your family doctor or a nutritionist beforehand, to make sure you're preparing foods safely and introducing them at appropriate times.

BOTTOM LINE: Expect to save about $2 a day during baby's first year.

➤ **Make your own baby wipes.** Baby wipes have perhaps the shortest and most inglorious lifespan of any consumer product. You can easily and cheaply make your own by cutting a roll of paper towels in half and placing the towels in a plastic container with 2 cups of water, 2 tablespoons of liquid baby bath soap and a bit of baby oil. When they're thoroughly soaked, remove the cardboard tube. You can also make washable wipes with baby washcloths.

BOTTOM LINE: Eliminate the need for buying refill packages at $8 per 200 wipes.

➤ **Save coupons and samples.** Diapers, formula and other expensive staples are often promoted with in-store coupons and samples handed out in doctor's offices. Ask friends and families to save these for you and make a point of stocking up when you find a good coupon, even if you have to visit the same store three days in a row to get around the one-per-customer rule.

BOTTOM LINE: Score a week's worth of formula and save $25.

Save on Birthday Parties

If you have childless friends, ask them how much they think a child's birthday party costs today. Chances are they'll be bowled over to learn that middle-income parents can spend over $200 on a six-year-old's bash. The peer pressure and one-upmanship is undeniable, but it is possible to hold a birthday bash on a budget. Here are some parent-tested tips:

- If you're older than 30, chances are high that you had most of your own childhood birthday parties at home. Older kids may balk at home parties today ("Mom, that's so *lame*"), but they can still be great for younger ones. You can entertain toddlers and school-agers with low-cost activities like dress-up games (pick up a bag of items at a thrift store), face painting and crafts.

- Here's a great idea for a super-cheap teen party: have a scavenger hunt at the mall. Partygoers get a list of items they have to collect, write down or shoot with their digital cameras. Some examples: a photo with a security guard, tacky jewellery from a coin-operated machine, a coloured plastic spoon. Just make sure you establish clear ground rules for behaviour ("no shoplifting" comes to mind).

- Anyone can bake a simple birthday cake from a mix, for a fraction of the cost of buying one from a bakery. If you're good in the kitchen, get creative and decorate it according to your child's favourite sport or TV or movie character. There's a ton of ideas online at sites such as easy-birthday-cakes.com and coolest-birthday-cakes.com.

- If your child has a summer birthday, have a party at a local park. Splash pads are ideal if your park has one—just make sure to call the town hall to make sure the water will be running at party time. Otherwise, kids can play soccer, basketball, Frisbee or other sports. Bring a boom box, pack the cake in a cooler and enjoy the outdoors.

- Buy toys and games at clearance sales and keep them in a special box. When your child is invited to a party, pick the most appropriate item for the birthday boy or girl. Don't be afraid to re-gift! If your child gets a book or toy he already has (or that he doesn't like), add it to the box and pass it along to someone else. Just make sure to attach a note reminding you where the gift came from so that you don't accidentally return it to its original owner!

- If your child has a friend with a birthday in the same month, ask the parents whether they would be willing to have a joint party and split the cost. This works especially well if the kids are in the same class and have many friends in common. However, it can create an awkward situation for the parents of invitees, who may feel obliged to buy two gifts. If both birthday kids are on board, consider asking partygoers to bring a single donation to a favourite cause, such as an animal shelter or toy drive.

- Save on expensive invitations by making your own. Pick up 3 x 5 index cards at the dollar store. Help your birthday boy or girl paint the unlined side a shiny colour, let it dry and decorate with glitter, stickers or whatever your child likes. Then write the party info on the lined side. Or you can encourage your child to design and print her own invitations on the computer.

- Sure, you can save on expensive loot bags by picking up trinkets from the dollar store, but who wants to add to the piles of junk everyone already has? Instead, come up with innovative party favours. An example: have the kids decorate an inexpensive picture frame, then snap a digital photo of each child with the birthday girl, print them on the computer and put them in the frame. ■

➤ **Forget brand names for babies.** Your little one doesn't care whether she's wearing Baby Gap or Zellers, and she certainly doesn't need brand-name shoes before she can crawl. Save the label-consciousness for her teen years and focus on buying the type of clothing your baby will be wearing most: good-quality undershirts and sleepers that will hold up to many washings.

BOTTOM LINE: Baby clothes with prestigious labels can easily be three times the cost of quality outfits from a department store—even switching from Baby Gap to Old Navy can save you $10 on an infant T-shirt.

➤ **Buy bigger sizes.** To get the most out of your baby-clothing budget, don't buy items that your bundle of joy will outgrow in a couple of months. Most kids' clothing is smaller than the labels suggest: an average-sized six-month-old can happily wear duds labelled "9 to 12 months." Even if the clothes are roomy at first, babies grow quickly. If you spot a great deal on clothes that are bigger than your baby can use now, buy them anyway and stash them until they're needed.

BOTTOM LINE: Save 30% to 50% if you plan several months ahead and buy only when clothes are on sale.

➤ **It's OK to accept hand-me-downs—especially if they're brand names.** If a relative or neighbour has a well-dressed child who is older than yours, drop a hint that you're open to accepting hand-me-downs. (Sometimes people are reluctant to offer, for fear you might feel insulted.) Name-brand clothes usually hold up well, so kids typically outgrow them before they wear them out. And many kids would rather wear previously enjoyed clothes from Hollister or American Eagle than new stuff from the Wal-Mart clearance rack. Even preteen girls are often happy to accept cool clothes from an older kid they look up to, especially non-intimate items like a jacket or handbag.

BOTTOM LINE: Inheriting a gently worn Abercrombie & Fitch hoodie will save you $50.

➤ **Stick to clothing basics.** Two-piece outfits look cute, but it's frustrating when your child outgrows or tears the knee of the pants, making the matching top useless. When shopping for little-kid wardrobes, think about mixing and matching. Choose primary colours and simple styles for shirts and pants so you can create several combinations from a few basic items.

BOTTOM LINE: A two-piece outfit from a baby boutique can top $40, while the same amount can buy you several well-made coordinating tops and pants at a department store.

➤ **Find a good consignment shop.** Kids outgrow clothes at a dizzying pace, and it won't be long before you have boxes of too-small togs. If you aren't planning to have another child, open an account with a local consignment shop that will sell your child's clothes and give you a portion of the price. (Many take used toys and books, too.) If the consignment shop sells adult clothing, you can bring in items you no longer wear and use the credit toward clothes for your baby. Some people even pick up items at garage sales and sell them at consignment shops for a profit.

BOTTOM LINE: If you buy quality kids' clothes and look after them, you can recoup a couple of hundred bucks a year.

➤ **Buy clothing at the end of the season.** This one takes some forward thinking, but the payoff can be huge, especially on expensive items like coats and boots. Most stores offer deep discounts on winter clothing in February and March: buy one size bigger than your child wears now and put it aside until next year. You can also find similar deals at the very beginning of winter, when retailers try to offload last year's styles to make room for new inventory.

BOTTOM LINE: Time things right and you can pick up a $100 snowsuit for half price.

➤ **Collect points.** In addition to collecting rewards from Aeroplan and Air Miles, sign up for loyalty programs at the stores where you buy kids' stuff. Many major Canadian retailers have point-collection programs, such as Sears Club and Hbc Rewards (from The Bay, Zellers and Home Outfitters). Maximize the benefit by shopping on bonus days: if you buy diapers at Shoppers Drug Mart, wait for the promotional events that offer 20 times the Optimum points. If you spend $200 (it doesn't have to be all at the same time), you can redeem the points for $75, for a savings of almost 40%. Even small retailers offer loyalty incentives—some kids' shoe stores, for example, will give you every fourth or fifth pair free. And don't forget grocery stores and the gas station where you fill up the minivan. **BOTTOM LINE:** If you frequent the same stores week in and week out, you can save hundreds of dollars annually redeeming your rewards.

➤ **Reduce your losses.** Visit the lost-and-found at your child's school and you'll find enough hats, mitts, gym shorts and shoes to clothe a small nation. If your child routinely loses stuff, invest in a container of iron-on or stitch-on nametags that will help lost items make their way home again. Or simply buy a laundry marker and write his name somewhere discreet. (If your child thinks this is dorky, make it clear that any lost clothing will be replaced out of his allowance or birthday money.) If your kids attend summer camps where losses are inevitable, buy a "camp wardrobe" at a thrift shop so you won't get worked up when some of it disappears.

BOTTOM LINE: A couple of bucks for a permanent marker will pay for itself many times over if it rescues just one pair of shoes.

➤ **Take the tax breaks for child care.** The federal government allows dual-income families to deduct child care expenses, including daycare, nursery programs and summer camps. You can also deduct any money you pay to a neighbour or relative over age 18 who watches your kids while you work, but you'll need a receipt. You can deduct up to $7,000 a year for kids under 7, and $4,000 annually for older kids up to 16. In most cases, the spouse with the lower income must take the deduction.

BOTTOM LINE: If you earn $40,000 a year, reducing your taxable income by $7,000 puts $1,600 to $1,900 back in your pocket, depending on which province you live in.

➤ **Trade child care.** Organize a babysitting co-op in your neighbourhood: by watching other people's kids, you earn points you can redeem for child care when you need it. Search the web for "how to start a babysitting co-op" for a long list of articles to get you going. Or, if you work part-time, try to find another parent with an opposite schedule and watch each other's children when you're not working.

BOTTOM LINE: The going rate for teenage babysitters can be as much as $10 an hour, so the co-op route can save you around $20 on a night at the movies.

➤ **Discover homemade toys.** You don't have to be an elf to make simple toys. Young kids love homemade playdough (mix 2 cups of baking soda, 1 1/2 cups of water, 1 cup of cornstarch and a little food colouring), shakers made with containers and dried beans, magnetic fishing ponds or simple sorting games made from recipe cards. Bigger kids can make cool stuff like a marshmallow gun for a couple of bucks' worth of PVC pipe. Troll the web for dozens of ideas and instructions.

BOTTOM LINE: Save the $40 you'd spend on a tub of Lincoln Logs by making a set of blocks from the mouldings left over from a reno project.

➤ **Make your own Halloween costumes.** Store-bought costumes can be absurdly expensive. With some imagination and a trip to the thrift shop and the dollar store, you can make your own. Look online for dozens of great ideas. A young child could be a clown, a hippie, a bunny, a pirate or a mummy. An older kid can go with a character from a teen book, such as a vampire from the *Twilight* series, or a movie—*Napoleon Dynamite* and *Juno* have been popular in recent years.

BOTTOM LINE: A homemade costume will come in $30 to $50 cheaper than a store-bought superhero.

➤ **Buy once, refill often.** Kids love hand soap, bubble bath and other personal hygiene items that come in containers decorated with their favourite TV or Disney characters. But instead of buying these overhyped and overpriced items regularly, buy them once and then top them up with generic refill bottles. You can even add a little water to liquid soap to stretch it further and make it easier to lather.

BOTTOM LINE: You'll pay more than $4 for a 250 mL bottle of hand soap if it has a kiddie design. Generic soap in a refill bottle (1.5 to 2 L) works out to less than one-sixth of that price.

➤ **Buy holiday gifts a year early.** You can reduce your holiday budget enormously by stocking up on toys and kids' clothing when it goes on sale immediately after Christmas. This is also the best time to get decorations, ornaments, cards and wrapping paper. For nieces, nephews and other little family members, keep an eye out for sales all year and stash the loot until the holidays.

BOTTOM LINE: Wait until January and you can expect savings of up to 75% on anything with a Christmas theme.

➤ **Buy school supplies in summer.** Unlike calendars and day planners, which end up in bargain bins as soon as the new year begins, school supplies are actually cheaper before the academic year starts. Stores compete hard to get your back-to-school business, so August is the time to buy the supplies your kids will need, such as pencil crayons, notebooks and binders, math sets and a dictionary. Back-to-school sales are also the best time to buy pricier items like knapsacks.

BOTTOM LINE: In the long run it's better to pay $30 for a good-quality backpack on sale than to buy a cheaper one that won't last the year.

➤ **Give personalized teacher gifts.** Teachers love to be appreciated, and the good ones deserve lavish praise from kids and their parents. Gifts are a nice gesture during the holidays and at the end of the school year, but teachers secretly admit they don't use half the stuff they get from their students. Forget the "World's Greatest Teacher" travel mug, the scarf and the stationery that no one has used since email. Instead, have your child write a personal card and give it to her teacher with a dozen home-baked chocolate chip cookies.

BOTTOM LINE: Save the $20 you would have spent on a traditional gift.

➤ **Explore new interests slowly.** If your child wants to play the drums, you don't need to immediately buy a new kit and sign her up for three months of lessons. Consider renting an instrument first, or borrowing one from a family who has gone through it all before. If you do sign up for lessons, don't commit to anything long-term until you know your child is genuinely keen.

BOTTOM LINE: Long & McQuade, a national chain of music stores, will rent you a $450 drum kit for just $25 a month.

➤ **Set limits on activities.** Kids love to try new activities, and parents should nurture this desire. But that doesn't mean you have to sign them up for soccer, softball, dance, horse-back riding and piano all at the same time. Multiple activities are a huge strain on the family purse, and busy kids can be stressed out and surly. Consider allowing your kids only one extracurricular activity per season, and encourage them to spend more time practising their chosen sport or skill.

BOTTOM LINE: With music and dance lessons costing $100 a month or more, cutting out the weekly sessions for an overprogrammed pianist or ballerina can save over $1,000 annually.

➤ **Organize an equipment exchange.** Sports equipment—especially hockey gear—can cost a few hundred dollars a year, and your kids will outgrow it quickly. Talk to your local sports league about organizing a used-equipment sale where parents can buy and sell gently worn skates, helmets (make sure they're in good condition) and other items or trade them for larger sizes. As a bonus, you can donate leftovers to organizations that collect sports equipment for those in need.

BOTTOM LINE: Pick up a composite hockey stick from an older child who's outgrown it and save at least $50. Unlike wood sticks, composites can easily last two seasons of minor hockey.

➤ **Carpool with other sports parents.** If your child's schedule is filled with hockey or dance practices, ask other parents if they're willing to split the driving duties. Even a small vehicle will do the job for two adults and two kids, and if parents are willing to skip practices when they're not behind the wheel, you can even divide the miles among three or more families. Successful carpooling requires everyone to share the job more or less equally, so don't skimp at the other parents' expense.

BOTTOM LINE: The Canadian Automobile Association estimates that driving a minivan costs more than 15 cents per kilometre. Knock just 20 km a week off your odometer and you'd save almost $160 annually.

➤ **Find creative ways to save on treats.** Summertime isn't the same without frozen treats, but heading out for a cone at Baskin-Robbins every week can leave you cold. For young children, simple and inexpensive freezies are just as good as gourmet ice cream. If your kids like canned fruit, save the juice, add a little water and pour it into funky ice-cube trays (available at dollar stores). For older kids and adults, freeze individual containers of yogurt: you can even buy plastic "handles" that make them easier to enjoy.

BOTTOM LINE: Substitute homemade frozen goodies for a trip to Baskin-Robbins or Dairy Queen and a family of four will save $10 a trip.

➤ **Forget convenience foods in the lunchbox.** Making kids' lunches can be a chore, and it's tempting to look for convenience foods that save time. But you pay dearly for gaining perhaps a few minutes a week. Give up those individually wrapped pieces of cheddar, pre-sliced apples and other pricey lunchbox items. Save a bundle by taking a few minutes a day to make up your own portions and roll them in plastic wrap or snack-size resealable bags (which you can wash and reuse).

BOTTOM LINE: You pay big time for convenience. Single-serving packages of baby carrots and dip cost about $1 each. That same $1 can buy a one-pound bag of the exact same carrots—about one-seventh the cost.

➤ **Stretch your dollar at kid-friendly restaurants.** Look for restaurants that offer free extras. For example, East Side Mario's doles out all-you-can-eat soup or salad and bread with many entrées, which goes a long way if you share. Bottomless drink refills are also a must if you can't enjoy a restaurant meal without pop or an after-dinner coffee. Many restaurants have "kids eat free" nights, and community newspapers and magazines often include two-for-one coupons for local eateries.

BOTTOM LINE: One free entrée can reduce your bill by $10 or $15.

➤ **Watch those drinks.** Restaurants make much of their profit on pop and alcohol. If you enjoy the convenience and fun of eating out with kids, encourage them to drink water with their meals. You can set an example by forgoing your glass of wine, and save even more. Here's a tip for families with a small child who uses a sippy cup: order milk or juice for yourself and fill her cup from yours.

BOTTOM LINE: Knocking two or three glasses of chocolate milk or Coke off the bill can save you $6 to $8 every time you dine out. Skip one glass of wine or pint of beer and save another $6 or $7.

➤ **Keep a stash of treats.** No parent likes to admit it, but we've all bought our kids candy or cheap toys just to keep them quiet while on a shopping trip or family outing. To avoid the expense of these impulse buys, keep a secret stash in your purse or in the car. Kinder Surprise eggs are much cheaper when you buy them in bulk, for example, and they can save the day with little ones. So can stickers or puzzle books you pick up at the dollar store.

BOTTOM LINE: Pocket $100 a year if you can save $2 on your weekend errands.

➤ **Brown-bag it on road trips.** When you pack the kids in the car for a trip to the cottage or a visit with out-of-town friends, take along a cooler with lunch and snacks so you don't have to stop for expensive (and unhealthy) fast food. If you can't find a rest area on your route, stop at a restaurant with outdoor seating, buy a drink or two to satisfy the management, and break out your picnic.

BOTTOM LINE: A home-packed lunch for a family of four can be $25 cheaper—and much more nutritious—than stopping at McDonald's.

➤ **Have a family movie night.** Instead of going to the cinema, rent a DVD (or borrow one from the library or a friend) and have a home movie night. To make this work, buy into the movie atmosphere: dim the lights, snuggle on the couch with a bag of microwave popcorn (you'll save $6 right there) and don't get up to do put the clothes in the dryer or answer the phone until the show is over. This also works great for teens, though you may have to encourage them with a home-baked treat and a promise to stay out of their hair.

BOTTOM LINE: For two kids and two adults, a movie at the cineplex plus drinks and popcorn will have you dropping $50 before the first car commercial hits the screen.

➤ **Membership has its privileges.** You can save a bundle on family outings by purchasing a membership or season pass at theme parks, museums and zoos instead of buying individual tickets every time you visit. Many places will allow you to apply the cost of one day's tickets toward a membership, which gives you a chance to check things out and decide whether you'll want to come back.

BOTTOM LINE: You can save hundreds if you visit a favourite attraction several times in a year. At the Royal Tyrell Museum in Drumheller, Alberta, for example, a family of four pays $32 for one admission, while a family membership costs just $60 and is good for a year's worth of visits.

➤ **Swear off gift shops.** Family outings to museums, the zoo or a theme park are expensive enough without the ritual trip to the gift shop, where kids will nag you to buy a knick-knack they'll never use. Make it a family policy to skip the souvenir buying after day trips. Instead, bring along a new book or inexpensive toy and pull it out before you get in the car for the drive home.

BOTTOM LINE: Gift shops can suck $20 out of your wallet before you know what hit you.

➤ **Discover the library beyond books.** Parents of avid readers discover the library early on. But many overlook the selection of videos, music and magazines in the children's collections at their local branch. While buying or renting favourite DVDs is fine if your children will watch them over and over, borrowing them from the library is a great way to preview them for free. Older kids can also take advantage of the computer games and Internet access offered for free at some libraries.

BOTTOM LINE: Borrow one video a month and save $60 a year on rentals.

➤ **Hand over some of the decision making to your kids.** Many label-aware kids are simply oblivious to how expensive their preferences are. Why wouldn't they choose brand-name clothes over cheaper alternatives when it's not their money? Instead of constantly saying no, give your tweens and teens a realistic clothing budget and let them decide how to spend it—with a little guidance from you, of course. When they have to determine the trade-offs ("Do I buy the cheaper top and use the extra money for accessories?"), they may surprise you with their bargain-hunting prowess. Plus, they'll learn a lesson about living within their means.

BOTTOM LINE: Letting your teens and tweens make their own choices will keep you on budget, saving you not only hundreds of dollars but also big headaches!

➤ **Get the card.** Teens can save on clothes and food with a Student Price Card, which many high schools hand out for free. If yours doesn't, you can buy one for $8.50: check out the website spclive.com for a list of retailers that sell it. When your teens flash the SPC card at participating stores and restaurants—including The Bay, Foot Locker, Campus Crew, Second Cup and Harvey's—they can save 10% to 15% on their purchases.

BOTTOM LINE: Reduce the damage by $15 or $20 during a single trip to the mall.

➤ **Pore over your teen's cell phone bill.** If you can get away with saying no to a cell phone for your teen, more power to you. If not, make sure you're getting the best deal you can. Most teens send text messages far more often than they make calls, so unlimited messaging is a must if you want to avoid death by a thousand cuts. Consider making your teen pay for her phone out of her allowance so she appreciates how the costs add up.

BOTTOM LINE: Unlimited messaging for $15 a month is a steal compared with 15 cents for each incoming and outgoing text.

➤ **Be smart about your child's computer.** Having a computer and Internet in the home is pretty much a necessity today, but paying top dollar isn't. Opt for a refurbished or second-hand computer, with some inexpensive upgrades if necessary. Make use of the free (and completely legal) software available online from sites such as download.com. Antivirus software (free versions are available) will also save you from costly repairs—not to mention data loss—especially if your child uses virus-prone MSN and file-sharing programs.

BOTTOM LINE: Open Office is the best deal going for any students in your home. This completely free suite of programs includes a word processor, spreadsheet and presentation program that mimics PowerPoint. (Download it from openoffice.org.) Compare that with the $150 price tag on the student version of Microsoft Office.

➤ **Claim the Tuition Tax Credit.** If your child earns income from a part-time job or from investments, she may be able to reduce or eliminate taxes by claiming the Tuition Tax Credit. Students can claim this non-refundable credit for any tuition they pay to college or university, including those outside Canada. If your student doesn't need the tax credit because she has little or no income, a parent can claim it instead. Check the Canada Revenue Agency website (cra-arc.gc.ca) for details.

BOTTOM LINE: Unless she has a very lucrative job or huge portfolio, a student enrolled in full-time studies can typically reduce her tax bill to zero.

Claim All Child and Family Benefits

Make sure you are receiving all of the government benefits you're eligible for. If you're a couple, the parent who has primary responsibility for the kids should start by visiting the website cra-arc.gc.ca/benefits and filling out the Canada Child Tax Benefit application. Here's a quick guide to the major benefits:

- The Canada Child Tax Benefit is available to families with a child under 18. You should apply as soon as your child is born. The basic benefit is $108.91 a month per child (except in Alberta, where it varies with age), plus a supplement if you have three kids or more. The benefit gets reduced if your family net income is more than $37,885.

- The National Child Benefit Supplement is an additional payment for low-income families. It ranges from $168.75 per month for one-child families to $142 per month if you have three or more kids. It is reduced when your family net income exceeds $21,287.

- The Universal Child Care Benefit is a $100 monthly payment for families with children under six. It does not get clawed back according to your income.

- The Working Income Tax Benefit is a refundable tax credit for low-income families who are employed or seeking to enter the workforce. Families with employment income between $8,095 and $21,569 are eligible, and the maximum benefit in most provinces is $1,019 ($1,422 in British Columbia).

- The GST/HST Credit offsets the sales tax that low-income families pay on goods and services. For example, families with one child and a net income of $30,000 receive a $611 credit.

  The provinces and territories also offer their own child and family benefits. The Canada Revenue Agency website has all the details. If your family income is above the national average, your savings will be minimal, but low-income families can net several thousand dollars a year. ∎

CHAPTER 12

Bathroom

Bathrooms are a land of hidden costs. Because we're not buying big-screen TVs or expensive furniture for them (well, most of us, anyway) we often don't think about saving money in the loo until we're renovating. But bathrooms serve a huge function in our lives and are a great place to save big money through small changes, no matter whether you use yours as a utilitarian space to get ready in the morning or as a spa-like retreat at the end of the day. Whether you're a power showerer or a calm bather—or a bit of both—there are many ways to save money in the bathroom.

Reducing the amount of water you use in your bathroom can be an easy and inexpensive way to save some cash while getting clean. Inexpensive cost-cutting measures range from changing your washing routine to replacing your conventional showerhead with a low-flow model. For those looking for longer-term savings, look to replace your old toilet with a dual-flush model.

The upfront costs for saving water in your bathroom are low, but the water and energy savings can be significant.

➤ **Turn the water off when using the sink.** Keeping the warm water running while brushing or washing is like pouring money down the drain. Reduce your energy and water consumption for free by filling a sink and splashing away.

BOTTOM LINE: Changing the way you brush your teeth, wash your face or shave can save a family of four almost $50 a year in reduced water and energy consumption.

➤ **Take shorter showers.** Long, hot showers can add up to hundreds in extra energy use over the year. Change your shower habits and save money by shortening your steam time by 1 to 5 minutes. Some über-frugalists use a timer or stopwatch to reduce shower time, while others turn off the shower completely while lathering up. Some of these showering measures may be too extreme for your hygiene routine, but keeping an eye on the time you spend in the shower can help you save.

BOTTOM LINE: Reducing your showering time by just 5 minutes each day could add up to hundreds in savings over a year for a small family.

➤ **Choose showers over baths.** Which uses more water, your baths or showers? To determine for yourself if showering saves more water than bathing, plug the drain during your shower to see how much water is used and how it compares to your baths. Generally, baths consume more water and energy than a 10-minute shower with a low-flow showerhead. If you love being a bathing beauty, you can reduce the expense of soaking by filling your tub only halfway and using cooler water. Or save the bath for weekend spa sessions and opt for showers during the week.

BOTTOM LINE: A 10-minute shower with a low-flow shower head can cut your hot water usage by half when compared with bathing, adding up to big savings over the course of a year.

➤ **Install a low-flow showerhead.** Replacing your conventional showerhead with a low-flow showerhead is the best method for saving water and energy in your bathroom. In many families, showers can be the largest drain on hot water, and with a conventional showerhead, even a 10-minute shower can use up to 200 litres of hot water. Switching to an inexpensive low-flow showerhead can reduce your water consumption from 20 litres per minute to as little as 5.5 litres per minute. Special nozzles prevent you from feeling this decrease in water flow—you use less water but still get the feeling of a full-force shower.

BOTTOM LINE: Switching from a conventional to a low-flow shower head costs as little as $15, but the payback is almost immediate. With a family of four taking nearly 1,500 showers a year, the savings could add up to over $100 annually on energy costs.

➤ **Install dual-flush toilets.** Along with flushing less often and not using your toilet to flush garbage, the

Canada Mortgage and Housing Corporation has found that installing a dual-flush toilet can save 67% or more water than conventional toilets in a family home. Dual-flush toilets have two buttons, one for a half flush and the other for a full flush, using 6 litres of water or less per flush (compared with 13 to 20 litres in an older toilet). Dual-flush toilets can be purchased for as little as $130 at home renovation stores.

BOTTOM LINE: Replacing your conventional toilet with a dual-flush model saves on water. Before canning your old toilet, hire a certified energy adviser through the Government of Canada's ecoENERGY Retrofit grant program to qualify for federal rebates totalling $50 for each new low-flush or dual-flush toilet. Many provinces and municipalities will match this rebate for a total refund of $100.

➤ Extend your lotions, soaps and shampoos with water.
Adding a little bit of water to your favourite skin lotions, soaps and shampoos can make them last longer. You could effectively double or triple the number of washings in a shampoo bottle by just using less and adding some water. Most of these products are concentrated with cleansers so you won't notice a difference in their effectiveness if you dilute them.

BOTTOM LINE: Make your beauty products go farther by adding a little bit of water to them. If you manage to save even one bottle each of shampoo, conditioner, body wash and moisturizer, that's easily an extra $25 in your pocket.

Lemon, Honey and Ginger Cold and Flu Remedy

Drinking enough fluids is a tall order when you are suffering from the sniffles or coughing from a cold. Along with keeping well hydrated, doctors advise getting plenty of rest to best conquer the common cold. While I can't help you get some sleep, I can offer my frugalicious cold remedy, which costs significantly less than packaged over-the-counter lemon drinks. The ingredients for this remedy are kitchen staples that may already be in your refrigerator waiting to help you feel better.

Ingredients
> Lemon
> Honey
> Ginger

Instructions
1. Grate a small chunk of ginger into your favourite mug. A bigger chunk makes a spicier remedy.
2. Add the juice of half a lemon. Grating in a little lemon zest adds some soothing zing to the mix.
3. Add a dollop of honey for some sweetness.
4. Fill your mug with boiling water and stir. Let steep for a few minutes.
5. Strain out the ginger bits if they're not your cup of tea. Leaving the grated ginger in the mix adds additional zing to zap colds and flu symptoms fast. ■

➤ **Brush and floss regularly.** Regular brushing and flossing, along with twice-yearly dental visits, is the primary way to prevent tooth decay and cavities. The cost of toothpaste, floss and toothbrushes is minimal, at under $15 for the lot, but the cost of extensive tooth decay is thousands. Even a small filling can cost $200 and may require replacing every decade, costing thousands over your lifetime. Regular flossing may even save you money on your dental cleanings, since you are charged for the time they take to complete—less plaque, fewer pennies.

BOTTOM LINE: Ignoring your dental health can be expensive. Take care of your choppers by brushing and flossing regularly and smile with your dental savings.

➤ **Clear your sinuses with a Neti pot.** If you suffer from allergies, congestion or sinus ailments and spend mega money on medications like decongestants, you may want to try an inexpensive Neti pot to clear your troubled passageways. A Neti pot looks like a tiny teapot with a small spout; it is used to rinse out the nasal cavities with warm salt water. Medical studies have shown nasal irrigation to be safe, with no problematic side effects as long as the Neti pot is kept clean. Don't turn your nose up at alternative solutions to expensive sinus problems. Neti pots have been used for centuries by various cultures to relieve congestion, reduce symptoms of allergies and reduce inflammation of the nasal passages and sinuses.

BOTTOM LINE: At $20 to $30 for a little pot, the Neti could save you upwards of $180 a year on various decongestants and other medications.

Home Spa Ideas from Your Kitchen

Going to the spa every once in a while is a fun way to kick back and enjoy some rest and relaxation. Most of us would love to treat ourselves to a spa day more frequently, but let's face it—the costs of all these treatments can reallly add up. As an affordable alternative, stay home and raid your kitchen to de-stress and pamper yourself any time. Many of the ingredients for these beautiful-body recipes are probably already stocked in your kitchen.

Love Your Locks: Avocado and Lemon Hair-Conditioning Treatment
1. Mix together 1 avocado, 1 tablespoon lemon juice and 1 teaspoon of sea salt until it becomes a smooth paste. This is a great way to use up your overripe avocados!
2. Massage treatment into your hair for 3 minutes to work it through from root to end.
3. Leave conditioner in for 20 to 30 minutes while soaking in the tub, reading a book or listening to music.
4. Rinse and shampoo to completely remove the avocado treatment.

Just Face It: Egg White Mask
Use a simple egg white to tighten your facial pores and remove toxins from your skin.
1. Take an egg and separate the white from the yolk. Save the yolk to cook with.
2. Beat the egg white for about 1 minute or until frothy.
3. Gently apply egg white mask to skin and let it dry for about 10 minutes.
4. Remove egg white mask with warm water.

Easy on the Eyes: Cucumber Compress
To relieve puffiness and revitalize the sensitive skin around the eyes, simply place a few cucumber slices over your tired eyes.

Full Body: Olive Oil Treatments
Skin: Save money on store-bought moisturizer by massaging a drop or two of olive oil into your skin. Apply an extra drop to your elbows and feet—or other rough, dry areas that need extra softening.

Hands and Nails: Treat your dry chapped hands at night by smoothing on a generous amount of olive oil before bed. Be sure to wear some light gloves to maximize absorption. For dry and brittle nails, soak your fingertips in a small bowl of olive oil. Store the oil and reuse it for future treatments.

Lips: Save money on name-brand lip balm by applying a tiny drop of olive oil to your chapped lips. This treatment works wonders to soften sore, cracked lips. ■

➤ **Ease a sore throat with a salt gargle.** Take a pass on sugary syrups and lozenges and save some sick cash by rinsing with a saltwater gargle. Just add half a teaspoon of salt to a glass of warm water, mix and then gargle away! This can soothe a rough scratchy throat while rinsing away bad bacteria.

BOTTOM LINE: Save $3 on a bag of lozenges by reaching for a soothing saltwater gargle for achy and scratchy throats.

➤ **Buy generic medicines over brand names.** Generic and brand-name medicines contain the same active ingredients.

The only differences between the two tend to be packaging, marketing and price! For example, a bottle of brand-name ibuprofen can cost $20, while an equivalent generic can sell for $14, and may even contain more tablets.

BOTTOM LINE: Save 30% to 50% by choosing generic medicines over brand names to cure whatever ails you.

CHAPTER 13

Laundry Room

It's tricky to say something clean and refreshing about a dirty chore like laundry. Few people enjoy sorting stinky clothing, attending to machines, folding, ironing and wondering how the dryer managed to eat yet another sock.

What most of us don't complain about, though, is the total cost of doing the wash. Unless you clean your clothing at a coin-operated laundromat, you won't see a single penny spent on the spin cycle. The costs for water and drying are absorbed into your utility bills, while the expense of detergents and other cleaning agents are probably hidden in your grocery budget.

The truth is, cleaning clothing can be expensive. If you add up the costs of energy, water and detergent, plus the wear and tear on your clothing and machines, you'll probably find you spend hundreds each year.

When I moved into my first apartment decades ago, I couldn't understand why my utility bills were so high. Other than a small television, a refrigerator and a few lights, I didn't think I was consuming a lot of electricity. Then I took a look at my laundry-washing habits. By washing my wardrobe in hot water and running everything through the dryer, I was burning through considerable energy just cleaning my clothes. By making a few small changes to how I did my wash, I was able to cut my laundry costs significantly, while still keeping my clothing smelling fresh and clean.

Once you look at your laundry costs, you too may be surprised at just how much you spend on washing clothing. By following a few tips, it's easy to save a significant amount on the weekly wash.

Laundry Detergent

When it comes to laundry detergent, it seems the choices are endless. Many brands boast superior cleaning power, technologically advanced ingredients and meadow-fresh smells. These brands can also be costly, ranging in price from 20 to 40 cents per load, and that's only if you stick to the minuscule recommended amounts. Before adding some soap to your wash, try these tips to save on your detergent bill.

➤ **Buy generics or store-brand detergent.** Name-brand detergents are much more expensive than store-brand equivalents, even though both do the same job. Brand-name detergents cost from 30 to 40 cents a load, while generics cost 20 to 30 cents per load. Why pay more for the marketing hype and packaging associated with a brand-name detergent when the end result for all detergents is cleaner clothing?

BOTTOM LINE: Stick with store brands and wash for 10 to 20 cents less per load—a savings of $41.60 per year if you do four loads each week.

➤ **Use powder instead of liquid detergent.** Powdered laundry soaps cost far less than the liquid variety. The cost of powdered detergent ranges from 20 to 30 cents per load, while liquid laundry soap costs from 30 to 40 cents per load. These seemingly small differences can add up to hundreds a year in lost money depending on the size of your family and the number of loads you wash. If you love using liquid to lessen the soap residue on your clothing, then try saving with powdered by filling your washing machine with water and powdered soap before adding your laundry. This method helps dissolve the detergent powder more evenly into your wash.

BOTTOM LINE: Save up to 50% on each load by switching from liquid to powdered detergent.

➤ **Don't overfill the liquid laundry cap.** If you're a liquid laundry washer, pay close attention to the measurements on the detergent cap before pouring for your next load. Liquid detergent is often concentrated (often called "Ultra"), but the majority of us use more than the recommended amount of liquid soap and literally wash money down the drain. On the back of the detergent bottle you'll find recommended amounts for varying degrees of dirty laundry. For a medium-sized load, many manufacturers suggest you fill the detergent cap to the first line. If you wonder why you never get the advertised loads per bottle, it's probably because you're overfilling the cap, maybe even to the brim.

BOTTOM LINE: Look for measurement lines printed on the inside or outside of the liquid laundry cap to prevent spending triple the amount per load.

➤ **Use baking soda to deodorize, remove stains and soften fabric.** Rescue the soda from your fridge and toss it into your wash to naturally deodorize stinky gear and smelly shirts. Baking soda is cheapest when purchased from an animal feed store for 50 cents per kilogram and can save you hundreds by replacing expensive stain removers and fabric softeners. Just add 1/4 cup (50 mL) of baking soda at the start of the rinse cycle for an economical fabric softener and odour remover. To treat grease stains before putting clothes into the wash, rub with a paste made of a 50/50 mix of baking soda and water.

BOTTOM LINE: Baking soda is an inexpensive way to remove stains and soften fabric, and saves you hundreds by replacing an arsenal of laundering products.

➤ **Use white vinegar to cut grease, whiten, brighten and remove residue.** Use white vinegar in your wash to help clean your dingy laundry. White vinegar can soften water, whiten whites and remove soap residue. Depending on the size of the load, add anywhere from 1/8 to 1/2 cup (25 to

125 mL) of white vinegar to the first rinse cycle. Your clothing will smell clean and fresh and you won't smell any vinegar after your clothing is dry.

BOTTOM LINE: A 4-litre bottle of generic white vinegar sells for only $1.50 and does the job of many brand-name laundry cleaners.

➤ **Add borax powder to boost cleaning or to clean diapers.** Borax is a natural mineral that can be used to enhance the cleaning power of your laundry detergent. Most supermarkets carry borax for about $4 for a 2 kg box. When added to your wash, borax is an antibacterial, water-softening, whitening wonder that stretches your detergent by boosting its cleaning power—allowing you to use less detergent. Borax is every new parent's best friend because when added to diaper washes it gets the dirty stuff cleaner while removing odours. Just add 1/2 cup (125 mL) to your wash to get cleaner laundry for less money.

BOTTOM LINE: For pennies a load, add borax to whiten your wash, soften your water and neutralize the stuff in baby diapers while using less detergent.

➤ **Whiten with sunshine and lemon.** Rather than using chemical bleaches to whiten your wash, hang your whites outside on a bright sunny day. The rays from the sunshine will naturally bleach your fabrics for free. For extra whitening power, soak your whites in a mixture of hot water and lemon juice before washing.

BOTTOM LINE: Use a 20-cent lemon and sunlight to naturally whiten and bleach your whites. It's nearly free and minimizes your use of chlorine bleach.

➤ **Make your own laundry detergent.** Making your own laundry detergent is a very frugal way to cut costs on your total laundry bill. The ingredients for homemade detergent cost only $2 per batch, adding up to only 3 cents per load. The cost for powdered generic and brand-name detergent ranges from 20 to 30 cents per load, while generic and brand-name liquid laundry detergent ranges from 30 to 40 cents per load. Doing the math, it's easy to see how making your own laundry detergent can save you hundreds of dollars.

BOTTOM LINE: See the feature "How to Make Your Own Laundry Detergent" for instructions on how to save laundry loonies on your weekly washing.

How to Make Your Own Laundry Detergent

Making your own laundry detergent is easy and cheap and saves you money over time.

Ingredients

> 1/3 bar of soap
> 1/2 cup (125 mL) washing soda (not baking soda!)
> 1/2 cup (125 mL) borax powder

Instructions
1. Grate the soap or chop into small pieces.
2. In a saucepan, melt soap in 6 cups (1.5 L) of water. Do not boil.
3. Slowly add washing soda and borax, stirring until dissolved.
4. Pour mixture into a 2-gallon (8 L) container.
5. Stir in enough warm water to fill the container.
6. Let mixture sit for 24 hours to set into a gel or liquid laundry soap.

Laundry Instructions
For every load of laundry, use 1/2 cup (125 mL) homemade laundry detergent for a total of 64 loads per batch. ■

Washing

The next time you take your wardrobe for a spin, try some of these easy methods for washing your clothing for less.

➤ **Load washer to capacity.** Doing half loads may feel productive but it's an inefficient and expensive use of your washing machine. Half loads use less water but they consume the same amount of power as full loads, costing you more to launder less. By saving up your laundry and filling your machine to capacity, you can save on both water and energy.

BOTTOM LINE: Fill your washing machine to capacity and save as much as $50 a year. One large load of laundry uses less energy than multiple smaller loads, plus you'll do less laundry while you're at it.

➤ **Adjust water levels to the load size.** If you're washing a partial load, make sure you set the water level to match the size of your load. Overfilling your machine with warm or hot water uses more energy and costs you additional dollars.

BOTTOM LINE: Washing a partial load in an excess of warm or hot water costs you at least $27 a year more than if you set your machine correctly, if you do three loads a week.

➤ **Use the shortest washing cycle.** Choose the shorter washing cycles for lightly to moderately soiled clothing, leaving the normal to heavy wash cycles for the really dirty stuff. Wash settings like the permanent press option use extra water for rinsing, which can add up to extra dollars spent if the clothing is only lightly soiled.

BOTTOM LINE: Opting for shorter wash cycles for less dirty laundry can save you around $30 a year on five loads per month.

➤ **Wash in cold water.** Get out of hot water and save big bucks on your energy bill by washing in cold water. Cold-water washing and rinsing is the easiest way to save money on doing laundry, as the majority of the cost is in heating the water. Look for detergents specially formulated for cold-water washing to get your clothing its cleanest.

BOTTOM LINE: By switching to cold-water from hot-water washing, the average family could save up to $27 dollars per year.

➤ **Use the right amount of detergent.** Adding too much detergent to your wash makes your machine work harder and is a waste of money. Rather than pouring excess detergent down the drain, read the recommended amount on your detergent package and review the manual for your washing machine to learn what amount of soap is required for hard or soft water. Contact your local water utility to find out how hard or soft your water is.

BOTTOM LINE: Adding too much laundry detergent to your wash wastes money on soap but also makes your washing machine work harder. This costs you in increased energy consumption and could cost you even more by prematurely wearing out your washing machine.

➤ **Switch to a front-loading washer.** If you're shopping for a new washing machine, take a spin with an ENERGY STAR front-loading washer to save water, energy and detergent. ENERGY STAR front-loading washers start at $1,000 and can cost thousands more for premium brands. New washers are not cheap, so if your current machine is in good condition, then take a pass on a new one until the old one is washed up.

BOTTOM LINE: Investing in a new front-loading washer can decrease your water consumption by 40% to 50% and your energy costs by up to 60%.

➤ **Sort, invert, zip and bag to prolong clothing life.** The simple act of sorting your whites from colours, turning your clothing inside out, zipping zippers and placing delicates in a mesh laundry bag before washing can preserve fabrics and make your wardrobe last longer. Sorting fabrics and washing whites separately from colours keeps fabric dyes from bleeding and staining lighter coloured fabrics. Washing rough, heavy clothing separately from delicates protects fragile fabrics from getting snagged by durable clothing like jeans. Turning clothing inside out prevents the exterior of the fabric from being exposed to the friction from the machine and from other fabrics. Fastening snaps and doing up zippers on pants or jackets helps maintain the shape of some garments and prevents clasps and zippers from snagging in the washing machine. Quality mesh laundry bags cost around $3 to $5 and can last for years. Mesh bags protect fabrics from undue wear from machine rubbing and agitation with other fabrics in the wash. Clothing protected in mesh bags is less likely to be stretched or harmed during the spin, wash and rinse cycles.

BOTTOM LINE: Properly sorting and preparing your clothes before washing them preserves the value of your wardrobe and keeps you looking fabulous for less.

➤ **Hand wash delicates.** Hand wash your delicate garments, like hosiery, panties and bras, to extend fabric life and keep them looking new. Washing machines can be hard on delicate or structured garments, tearing them even when they're in mesh laundry bags. To hand wash, just fill a sink with cold water and carefully wash with some gentle soap, then let soak for 10 to 15 minutes. Rinse in cold water. Without wringing, gently squeeze water from clothing. Gently roll the garment in a clean, light coloured towel to absorb excess water. Hang to dry.

BOTTOM LINE: Hand washing delicate and fragile garments can keep them looking new and prevents them from getting damaged in the washing machine, saving you the cost of replacing your wardrobe.

Frugal Stain Removal Guide

Maintaining your clothing by acting fast to fight stains can save you hundreds each year in not having to replace your garments. Brand-name stain removal potions and lotions are expensive, and often don't remove stains any better than inexpensive household items. Try some of these frugal stain removers to save you some clothing bucks.

General tips

- Dab small spots with a cotton swab. Dab larger spots with a paper towel or clean washing towel.
- Some garments may need to be dry cleaned, so be sure to check the label.
- Mild liquid dishwashing soap such as Dawn costs $2 to $3 for a bottle and does wonders for removing stains.

Blood. If you have small children who scrape elbows and knock knees, chances are you have blood stains to launder. Blood stains can set and become permanent, especially if exposed to the heat in hot water or a clothes dryer. Prevent blood from staining clothing by treating it as soon as possible.

- Rinse with cold water.
- Spit on the stain, add salt and rub it in. The enzymes in your saliva will help remove the stain.
- Rinse again, and then wash in cold water.

Grass stains. Grass stains can be the most challenging stains to remove, especially from delicate fabrics. Avoid using ammonia, degreasers or alkaline detergents, which will set the stain permanently.

- Dab stain with rubbing alcohol. Repeat.
- Dab stain with vinegar. Let soak for 1 hour.
- Wash as usual. Do not put in dryer until stain is completely gone.

For extremely harsh grass stains. Warning: Use digestive enzymes only on cotton or synthetic fabrics. They will destroy silk and wool. You can buy human digestive enzymes at the drugstore for $7 for 90 capsules, enough to treat 45 grass stains.

- Mix a teaspoon of powder (crush pills or open capsules) with enough lukewarm water to make a paste; adding cold or hot water deactivates the enzymes.
- Apply to stain and let sit for 1 hour.
- Wash as usual.

Grease stains.

- Pre-treat the stain with a few drops of mild liquid dishwashing soap such as Dawn. Let sit for several minutes.
- Wash in the hottest water the garment will tolerate.

Lipstick.

- Scrape off any excess lipstick with a table knife. Take care not to smear it in further or spread it out.
- Dab—don't rub—stain with a clean white cloth soaked in rubbing alcohol (so you can see how much of the stain is being removed and also to prevent transferring colour from the cloth to the garment).
- Dab on mild liquid dishwashing soap such as Dawn. Let sit for a few minutes.
- Wash garment as usual, but do not put in dryer until the stain is completely gone. You may need to repeat this process a few times.

Red wine. Warning: Hydrogen peroxide may bleach some fabrics, so try on an inconspicuous area first.

- Mix equal amounts of hydrogen peroxide and a mild liquid dishwashing soap such as Dawn.
- Dab or pour carefully onto the stain.
- Blot with a clean cloth.
- Rinse with cool water. ■

Drying

Don't get hung out to dry with the expense of fluffing your fabrics. There are ways to get the most out of your dryer dollars with minimal effort. Or, to keep your savings spinning, try the natural alternative to dryers.

➤ **Hang dry your wet clothing.** Your clothes dryer uses almost as much electricity as your refrigerator. The easiest way to save on drying your clothes is to hang them to dry either indoors or outdoors. A wooden indoor clothes rack costs around $15 and can be used for years as an energy-efficient alternative to the clothes dryer, saving you hundreds. An outdoor clothesline could cost as little as $20 and uses the heat from the sun for free to quickly dry your laundry. Hanging your clothing to dry carries the added bonus of extending the life of your wardrobe by reducing fabric wear and shrinkage. If you prefer the feeling of fluffed towels or shirts, then place the wet items in your dryer for just 15 minutes on high heat, then pull them out while they're still damp and hang to air dry. Using a combination of fluff drying with a machine and hang drying on a rack can lead to considerable savings as well. Always hang clothing in areas with good air flow.

BOTTOM LINE: Hanging your laundry to dry is free and beats the operating costs of even the most efficient clothes dryers. Air drying your wash can save you hundreds a year depending on the size of your family and the volume of laundry. If you air dry four loads a week instead of using the dryer, you can save over $40 per year in electricity.

➤ **Remove dryer lint.** Cleaning the lint trap after each load can save you up to 30% on drying costs. A full lint trap doesn't allow moist air to escape properly, which slows down the drying cycle, which uses more energy.

BOTTOM LINE: By cleaning your dryer lint and debris from the lint trap after every load, you can save up to $25 in energy costs each year.

➤ **Don't mix fabrics when drying.** Drying light and heavy fabrics together, such as heavy sweaters and light T-shirts, dries up your dollars fast. Mixing dissimilar fabrics in the dryer prevents the fabrics from drying at the same speed, leaving the lighter fabrics damp.

BOTTOM LINE: Drying lighter and heavier fabrics in separate loads increases the drying speed for each load, saving you money.

➤ **Check your dryer's air vent.** Check your dryer's air outside vent to be sure it's venting well and free from obstruction. Good dryer ventilation is important for the efficiency and longevity of your dryer.

BOTTOM LINE: Check your dryer's outside vent and clear any leaves or debris that may compromise the machine's efficiency and longevity.

Frugal Alternatives to Dryer Sheets and Fabric Softener

Many frugal alternatives to commercial fabric softeners and dryer sheets will keep your laundry soft and static free. Here's how inexpensive common household basics can soften your sweaters and keep static from clinging to your socks.

Prevent static cling by not fully drying fabrics. Remove laundry from the dryer before it is completely dry. Static takes charge of your laundry during the last minutes of the drying process, so keeping a little bit of moisture in the fabrics keeps the cling away. Let the items finish drying on drying racks or the clothesline. Hang drying your laundry is free and saves you from spending $5.49 on a box of brand-name dryer sheets.

Dry natural and synthetic fabrics separately. In most cases the synthetic fabrics are to blame for causing static cling. Drying your natural fabrics separately from your synthetics can help reduce static cling. Alternatively, hang dry fabrics containing nylon, rayon and polyester to best prevent static. Hang drying will also increase the longevity of these fabrics.

Use white vinegar or baking soda as a fabric softener. Both white vinegar and baking soda are natural alternatives to chemical-based fabric softeners. Just add 1/4 cup (50 mL) of baking soda to your washing machine's first rinse cycle to soften fabrics. If you prefer white vinegar (don't worry, you won't smell it!), add 1/2 cup (125 mL) to the first rinse cycle.

Ironing

Save your wallet from getting flattened by ironing costs. The irony is that ironing can be done with less effort and for less money by using these simple pressing tips.

➤ **Iron less.** An average iron can draw over 1,000 watts of power, costing you 5 to 10 cents in electricity each hour. By purchasing clothing that does not require ironing, you can save time and money on ironing equipment and energy.

BOTTOM LINE: Going with the "wrinkly look" or buying "iron free" clothing can save you from buying ironing equipment and save energy costs. Ironing three hours less each month can save you around $4 each year and many hours of work.

➤ **Iron your own clothing**. Taking your shirts and pants to the cleaners can cost you big bucks over time, even dollars a shirt. Do your own ironing at home and reduce the costs of maintaining your wardrobe. An iron can cost as little as $20 and an ironing board about $40 to $120 depending on quality. If your garment is dry clean only, then do get a professional to launder your wares.

BOTTOM LINE: Buy an iron for $20 and save hundreds by ironing your own shirts. For example, ironing five shirts yourself each week instead of having them dry cleaned for $1.50 each or more can save you $390 a year.

➤ **Make ironing easier by removing clothing from the dryer while it's damp.** Ironing your favourite shirt or office pants is a lot easier when the fabric has not fully dried. Remove clothing from the dryer while it's still warm and a tiny bit damp, and then smooth it flat on a table. Leaving clothes in the dryer sets wrinkles, which require way more ironing time and costs more in energy consumption and patience. If some wrinkles do persist, get an inexpensive $3 spray bottle and spritz some water on the fabric. Spraying to moisten wrinkles helps to release folds and reduces pressing time. For clothes that are hung to dry, make sure you smooth all creases when hanging them on the rack.

BOTTOM LINE: Reduce your ironing time and energy consumption by smoothing flat slightly damp clothing rescued from the dryer early. Use a $3 spray bottle to soften already set wrinkles.

➤ **Remove creases by hanging garments in bathroom.** Pass on buying a clothing steamer and release wrinkles and creases from dried garments by hanging them in the bathroom while you shower. The steam will take out most of the creases for free.

BOTTOM LINE: Hang wrinkly clothing in the bathroom while you shower for free and save up to $150 by not purchasing a clothing steamer.

➤ **Use aluminum foil to reduce heat use**. Insert aluminum foil between the ironing board and the cover. The foil will reflect the heat back up through the garment, decreasing ironing time.

BOTTOM LINE: Use a $1 sheet of aluminum foil to conserve ironing heat and reduce ironing time.

CHAPTER 14

Garage

We always seem to be going somewhere, whether we're driving to work, commuting to school or heading out to the supermarket. Whatever your destination, the price you pay for transportation can be significant.

Most Canadian families own at least one vehicle, and even if you don't own the slickest set of wheels on the block, there's no doubt the sticker price for your ride was thousands of dollars. Buying a car is just one part of the expense, though. There's maintenance, insurance and fuel costs too, bringing the total cost of keeping a car on the road to thousands each year.

There are ways to get where you need to be for less. I made the ultimate automobile sacrifice years ago when I needed to drastically reduce my transportation costs—I sold my car and opted to walk, bike and bus to work daily. By renting an apartment close to work, I managed to commute inexpensively and saved thousands. While it might be financially ideal, living a car-free life is not an option for everyone. But there are numerous ways you can get your motor running and still save money on purchasing a new car, buying automobile insurance and filling up at the pump.

Your Car

➤ **Buy a smaller car.** A smaller car is not only cheaper to buy but will save you thousands in maintenance and operation costs over a year. The Canadian Automobile Association (CAA) publishes a yearly study comparing the costs of owning and operating larger and smaller vehicles. Check out the CAA online (www.caa.ca) to calculate the ownership costs of various vehicles—what seems like a minor difference can save you thousands each year.
BOTTOM LINE: According to the CAA, the annual operating costs of a larger Grand Caravan compared with a smaller Cobalt LT are 28% higher, while the average annual ownership costs are 33% higher. Driving a smaller car like the Cobalt LT will save you $2,800 a year if you drive 18,000 km a year.

➤ **Buy an off-lease used car.** The simple act of driving a sparkling new car off a dealership lot depreciates the value of your ride in seconds. Buy a quality used car from a reputable dealer and let someone else absorb thousands in losses. When buying a used ride, consider a three- or four-year-old vehicle that just came off its lease. Off-lease vehicles present the best value for your used-car dollar because they are scheduled returns to a manufacturer and are therefore less likely to have been in accidents or have mechanical issues. Used vehicles fresh off a lease are generally well maintained and are covered by the remainder of the manufacturer's warranty. Always have a mechanic you can trust inspect the vehicle before finalizing any decision.

BOTTOM LINE: Buying a used off-lease car saves you thousands in depreciation costs.

➤ **Pay cash when you buy an automobile.** While saving enough cash to purchase a house outright is a tall order for many families, saving enough to buy a vehicle in full is a possibility. Buying a car outright can save you hundreds, even thousands of dollars in car-loan interest while allowing compound interest on your savings to work in your favour. For example, buying a $15,000 car with a loan at 4.5% over five years costs you about $280 each month and totals $1,775 in interest, adding a whopping 10% to the total cost of that car. On the other hand, if you saved up to buy the car by putting $280 each month into a Tax-Free Savings Account (TFSA) at 3.5% interest, you'd save enough cash to buy the car outright in just over four years—paying off that car one year sooner than if you leased. By saving instead of borrowing, your total investment for the $15,000 car is only $13,775. That's $3,000 less than what you would pay with the loan.

BOTTOM LINE: It pays thousands to save a little money each month so that you can pay cash for big purchases like cars.

➤ **Lose the extra vehicle.** Get creative and optimize the use of a single-family vehicle to save huge money on insurance, gas, maintenance and car payments. You may be surprised with how many thousands of dollars can be saved by reducing the number of cars parked in your driveway.

BOTTOM LINE: By taking your savings from owning fewer cars and applying it to your mortgage, you could be mortgage-free five years sooner, saving you thousands more on interest over the years. For example, by cutting out one car and putting an extra $3,000 from insurance, fuel and maintenance against a $285,000 mortgage at 5% over 25 years, you may pay off the mortgage five and a half years earlier and save $51,285.19 in mortgage interest.

➤ **Maintain your vehicle.** Routine maintenance can save you a bundle by preventing major repair costs in the years to come. Follow your car's user manual to keep up-to-date with oil changes, replacement air filters and regular tune-ups. Keeping an eye on dents, parking in a garage overnight and doing routine rustproofing will keep you safe and increase the life of your ride, saving you thousands.

BOTTOM LINE: Regular maintenance makes your vehicle safer to drive and increases its longevity and fuel efficiency.

Gas

Filling up at the pump does a great job of emptying your wallet, but there are many things you can do to lighten your fuel consumption. Since gas prices swing wildly, they're also hard to budget for and to calculate—unless I've noted otherwise, all my tips assume a price per litre of 90 cents. Here's a trunkload of tips to keep you fuel frugal.

> ➤ **Drive less.** The most fuel-efficient vehicle is the one not running. A Hummer parked in the driveway consumes less fuel than a Prius driving on the road. By staying home Saturday nights, walking to the gym instead of driving, reading a book rather than motoring to the video store, and commuting using alternative transportation, you can save a lot of moolah on gas. You'll probably save money on doing more frugal activities at home as well.
> **BOTTOM LINE: Driving less or not at all saves you up to 100% on fuel costs.**

> ➤ **Replace air filters regularly.** A clogged or dirty air filter may reduce fuel mileage by up to 10%. A clean filter costs $30 to $100 depending on your car or truck size and prevents the engine from working unnecessarily hard by optimizing the air circulation in the motor. Labour to change a filter costs around $50 per hour, so read the manufacturer's manual and do this job yourself for free.
> **BOTTOM LINE: Replace your air filter every 24,000 km (or**

according to the manufacturer's recommendations) to increase your fuel mileage by 10%.

➤ **Keep tires properly inflated.** Make sure your tires are inflated to the manufacturer's recommended PSI. Low tire pressure not only results in increased wear on your car but it also reduces your gas mileage. To increase fuel efficiency, inflate tires to the higher pressure listed in the user manual— just don't go higher than the maximum pressure printed on the tire. Be warned, though: higher tire pressures will help save on gas but may result in a harsher ride on rough roads.
BOTTOM LINE: Check your tire pressure whenever you fill up at the pump and increase your fuel efficiency by 2%. This can save you just under 2 cents per litre.

➤ **Tune the engine.** Keep your engine running smoothly by regularly checking spark plugs, wires and fuel injectors and performing any necessary service. A smooth-running engine is much more efficient than one that may be misfiring or plugged because of overdue maintenance. A well-tuned ride could save you hundreds in fuel.
BOTTOM LINE: Get your engine running smoothly by regularly checking spark plugs and fuel injectors. Dirty old spark plugs can increase fuel consumption by as much as 30%.

➤ **Get the tires aligned.** You can improve fuel economy significantly by getting your tires aligned and properly balanced. Also check for any resistance on tires due to brake dragging and get them adjusted to reduce friction.

BOTTOM LINE: A smooth-running automobile with aligned tires and properly adjusted brakes may increase your fuel efficiency up to 20%—18 cents on every litre.

►**Combine trips.** Take a few minutes each day to strategically plan your daily trips and increase your savings on fuel dramatically. Lots of little stop-and-go errands can add up, and spinning your wheels all over town consumes your gas. Here are some tips to optimize your daily travel plans:

1. Start by listing all your fixed appointments.

2. Schedule all other non-fixed errands around your fixed appointments.

3. Plan your trip so the longest drive is done first. This tactic lets your car warm up properly and can increase overall fuel efficiency, more so than making several cold starts.

4. Get your car in gear and get everything done in one single trip. You may just find you'll end up saving both gas and time.

BOTTOM LINE: Planning your daily errands around one single trip can save you hundreds a year on gas and save you time as well.

► **Avoid accelerating heavily when city driving.** When driving in the city, you consume the most gas when you're accelerating. Because urban drivers constantly speed up and slow down during city jaunts, city cars have inferior gas mileage compared with highway cruisers. To save up to 50% on fuel consumption while driving in town, accelerate gently from a stop, leaving lots of space between your car and the one in front of you.

BOTTOM LINE: Adjusting your city driving habits to limit accelerating can cut your fuel costs by almost half—up to 45 cents per litre.

➤ **Slow down on the highway.** When cruising on the highway, your car burns lots of fuel just punching a hole in the air. While breaking wind may sound like fun, it's actually very expensive. The faster you drive, the harder your car has to work just to move forward against wind resistance. Because your car's work increases exponentially with the speed, slowing down by just 10% will save up to 10% in fuel costs, and will add a mere three minutes to a half-hour drive.

BOTTOM LINE: At typical highway speeds, slowing down 10% will save up to 10% in fuel costs over the same distance— saving you 9 cents per litre.

➤ **Reduce morning warm-up time.** An idling car is an expensive gas-guzzling machine. A car parked with the engine running can use anywhere from 1 litre to 4 litres of gas every hour going nowhere. Reducing the amount of time you warm up your car on cold winter mornings can save hundreds of dollars from going up in smoke. A good compromise is to start your car, wait a few seconds and gently drive off: modern cars warm up much faster and more efficiently when being driven than they do when idling.

BOTTOM LINE: Warming up your car for one hour less each month saves you up to $3.60 in fuel.

➤ **Stop idling.** Sitting in an idling car for 10 minutes waiting to pick up a friend burns through 0.2 litres of fuel. To save your gas money, consider turning your engine off if you're going to be stopped for more than 30 seconds. Many cities in Europe have installed countdown timers at longer lights to allow drivers to turn off their cars instead of sitting and idling—collectively saving our European neighbours hundreds of thousands in idle fuel costs each year.
BOTTOM LINE: Being idle while burning fuel in your car is a surefire path to watching your cash go up in smoke. An average car uses 0.2 litres of fuel for every 10 minutes of idling—which translates into $2.16 for every 2 hours of idle time.

➤ **Lose the roof rack.** Harness the power of aerodynamics and lighten your load by removing the unused roof rack on your car. On the highway, an empty roof rack will increase your fuel consumption by 5%. A roof rack loaded with bikes or a cargo box can add over 20%. Mount a roof rack only when it's needed and you can save a lot on gas.
BOTTOM LINE: Remove an unused roof rack to decrease fuel consumption by 5% and save 4.5 cents per litre.

➤ **Remove the extra junk in your trunk.** Are you packing lots of extra pounds in the trunk of your car? Every 100 pounds of extra weight in tow increases your fuel costs by 1% to 2% each time you drive up a hill or increase speed. Return overdue library books, toss out the trash behind the seat and remove the sandbags and chains from last winter. Not only will you save gas, you'll also feel happier driving in a clean vehicle. Just hang on to the spare tire to keep you safe.

BOTTOM LINE: Getting rid of 100 pounds of excess weight in your trunk lowers your fuel costs by 1% to 2%, a savings of 50 cents to $1 on a $50 tank of gas.

➤ **Try telecommuting from home.** Not everyone has a job or an employer who allows logging in from home, but if you do, try telecommuting. Working from home as little as one day a week can save one-fifth of your commuting gas, which effectively means you're getting paid a little bit more each week.

BOTTOM LINE: Save 20% on your commuting gas by logging in from home and telecommuting.

➤ **Do the math on buying a hybrid.** A hybrid is an automobile that uses two or more forms of power, generally an internal combustion engine and an electric motor. Driving a hybrid vehicle is an excellent way to improve fuel economy and cut down on pollution. But do hybrids save you money over a conventional car in the long run? The answer depends on which car you compare the hybrid with. For example, a hybrid Toyota Prius currently sells for $27,600, which is $10,000 more than a base-model Honda Civic. While the Prius hybrid easily uses 30% less fuel, these savings take years to recover based on the substantial price difference. Assuming 18,000 km per year with gasoline at $1 per litre, it would take more than 30 years of driving to make up the difference.

BOTTOM LINE: While buying a hybrid car may seem like the perfect solution to beating prices at the pump, consider the sticker price difference between the hybrid and the conventional car before laying out the extra dough to save on fuel.

➤ **Buy a more fuel-efficient vehicle.** If you own an older car or a large truck, it may be time to upgrade to a more fuel-efficient model. Driving a car like the Honda Fit could save you hundreds a year on fuel alone. For example, a Chrysler PT Cruiser uses about 8 litres of fuel per 100 km, while a Honda Fit burns only 6 litres. If you drive 18,000 km each year, you save $360 in fuel each year or a thrifty $1 each day (assuming gas is $1/L). Before buying a car, review the fuel efficiency ratings listed on manufacturers' websites. You may be surprised how much money you can save by comparing cars within the same class and cost range, so really do your homework before you buy.

BOTTOM LINE: Buying a fuel-efficient car like the Honda Fit rather than a bigger vehicle with a V8 engine results in savings of almost $1,000 per year.

➤ **Ditch the car and ride a bike, walk or take the bus.** Depending on where you live, going car free can be either a huge challenge or a thrifty reality. When I lived in Vancouver, I managed to commute without a car for 10 years and lived to tell the tale. The Government of Canada offers tax credits for people who hold transit passes for buses, streetcars, subways, commuter trains and local ferries. The amount you can claim depends on your income, so check out transitpass.ca to see your possible tax credits.

BOTTOM LINE: By walking or riding my bike to work each day, I saved at least $3,500 a year. That's $35,000 saved over 10 years—not including compound interest. These savings are equivalent to getting a free year off work.

➤ **Get in a carpool.** One vehicle travelling with four people consumes 75% less gas than four vehicles carrying one person each. Carpooling is an awesome method for increasing the number of butts sitting in your car while decreasing both the gasoline consumed and the number of vehicles on the road. Even if you carpool once weekly with just one other person, you will still save 10% of your commuting gas costs. Many cities have carpool or "high occupancy vehicle" lanes, which makes your commute both faster and cheaper. Check out Carpool.ca to arrange a carpooling group near you.

BOTTOM LINE: Save some stress and big dollars on gas by carpooling to work or school. Sharing a ride as little as once per week can save you 10% on commuting costs.

How to Track Your Gas Mileage

It's impossible to tell if your attempts to save on gas are actually successful without tracking and measuring your fuel consumption. Tracking your gas mileage doesn't require any fancy equipment or expensive gadgets. All you need is a notebook, a pen, an odometer, a gas receipt and some time to figure it out. Here are the free goods on calculating your fuel consumption.

1. **Fuel up.** Each time you fill your tank, write down the distance you drove on the last tank, the amount of fuel you just purchased and the price per litre.
2. **Clear trip odometer.** Reset your car's trip odometer to start measuring the distance before the next fuelling.
3. **Calculate.** When you get home calculate the fuel efficiency of that tank. Calculate your litres per 100 km by multiplying the total litres of gas used by 100, and then dividing that number by the total kilometres driven. For example, if you drove 450 km and used 44 litres, then your mileage is 9.8 L/100 km.
4. **Record.** Write these numbers in a notebook and keep it handy in your car. Periodically review the numbers to see if your attempts to improve mileage are paying off. ■

Automobile Insurance

➤ **Drive safely and get a better rate.** A safe driver will pay much less in insurance than an unsafe one. Insurance companies generally give discounts to drivers who have maintained a clean record for a number of years. Conversely, drivers with insurance claims and accidents on their record may pay more than triple the base rate.

BOTTOM LINE: Being an accident-free driver and keeping a clean record could save you hundreds a year on insurance premiums. Make sure you claim your reward for good driving by negotiating a good rate.

➤ **Shop around for insurance (if you can).** Drivers living in British Columbia, Saskatchewan, Manitoba or Quebec insure vehicles through their provincial public auto insurance company and have a set rate. Drivers living in other Canadian provinces and territories are insured privately and must shop around to find the best deal on auto insurance. With private insurance, rates can vary when factoring in the various discounts you may be eligible for. Get at least three quotes and compare packages before deciding on an insurance policy.

BOTTOM LINE: Living in a province with private automobile insurance gives you the opportunity to shop around for the best rate. Many insurance companies will offer discounts to groups like alumni or professional associations. Always ask for a better deal if you're a claim-free driver.

➤ **Match insurance to your needs.** Skip paying for extensive collision or comprehensive coverage if you drive an older automobile where the added insurance expense doesn't outweigh the replacement vehicle cost. For example, if your vehicle is worth $1,000 and your comprehensive insurance with a deductible costs $300, the most an insurance company might pay before writing off the car is around $700.

BOTTOM LINE: Don't pay for extensive collision or comprehensive insurance if your vehicle replacement value is close to the amount of the deductible.

➤ **Raise your deductibles.** Get out your car insurance policy and make the call to raise the deductibles by as little as $300 to $500 to save big money on insurance costs each year. Raising deductibles on cracked windshields or dents could save you hundreds on insurance each year and will probably more than offset the out-of-pocket costs of paying for minor fixes yourself. And by making infrequent claims on only big fixes rather than small scratches, you come out ahead by saving on additional insurance premiums.

BOTTOM LINE: Raising comprehensive and collision deductibles by $500 can save you up to 5% on your total automobile insurance premiums.

CHAPTER 15

Outside Your Home

If you grow it, you have to mow it. There's no doubt that culti-
vating a garden and maintaining a lawn can be costly. Routine
gardening activities like mowing grass, watering plants, growing
vegetables and planting flowers can add up to hundreds spent
each year just making your outdoor space greener.

But there's no need to sacrifice your plot of land to save some
green. Regardless of where you live or how much space you
have, you can love your lawn and watch your vegetable garden
grow for less by using the frugal techniques in this chapter to
cut costs while exercising your green thumb.

➤ **Plant perennials rather than annuals.** It seems counterintuitive to spend around $150 to grow a garden with
perennial plants rather than paying $30 for a flowerbed of
annuals. Looking longer term, though, perennial flowers are
the better deal because they grow back every year, whereas
the annuals lose their bloom after just one season. But if

you're a notorious plant killer, annuals might be a better investment!

BOTTOM LINE: Perennial flowers cost five times more than annuals, but save you hundreds over the years because they grow back every year.

➤ **Sow from seeds rather than buying plants.** Filling your garden with ready-grown plants provides instant gratification but it's far more expensive than sprouting from seeds. Planting 10 tomato plants for $3 a piece totals $30, while a packet of 20 seeds is around $5 with only a 25-cent cost per plant. Growing your garden from seeds in this case gives you twice the number of plants, and you'll have plenty of extras to replace those that don't survive.

BOTTOM LINE: By growing from seed instead of purchasing plants, you pay only a tenth of the cost for your garden. If you loved your flowers or vegetables from the previous year, then save your seeds for free and enjoy the fruits of your labour next year.

➤ **Save your seeds.** Many flower and vegetable varieties produce seeds that you can save and plant the next spring. Saving seeds may take a little bit of work, but you don't need to pay for plants next season, and you'll have a ready supply of your favourite hard-to-find varieties. Unless you're into experimenting, plant heirloom varieties each year. Hybrid flowers and vegetables generally produce plants significantly different from their parents, so you may be startled to see what sprouts from the seeds you saved from last year. Look online for plant-specific instructions on how to harvest seeds at the end of the season.

BOTTOM LINE: Save some gardening dollars by planting heirloom plants and saving the seeds for next year. By saving enough seeds to replace 10 packages at $2.50 each, you can save $25 a year and keep the varieties you like to grow.

➤ **Convert part of your lawn to a vegetable garden.** Adding green space around your home in the form of a lawn is attractive, but it's also expensive when you consider the costs of growing grass over the savings gained from having your own vegetable garden. By converting a portion of your greenery to a small vegetable garden, you get more bang for your soil buck and can save money on your food budget. If you have a bumper crop and grow too many veggies for a summer of salads, freeze or preserve them to enjoy inexpensive and healthy produce in the winter.

BOTTOM LINE: With a bit of care, a $3 tomato plant can easily yield 25 pounds of tomatoes by the end of the summer. At $1.50/pound, this is equivalent to more than $35 of store-bought tomatoes—plus they'll be tastier.

➤ **Plant expensive foods.** Use your garden space wisely by growing vegetables that are expensive to buy but easy to grow. Foods like broccoli, garlic and herbs can cost dozens of dollars at the supermarket. Freeze, dry or preserve your extras for the winter months.

BOTTOM LINE: Planting $5 of herbs from seeds in your garden and freezing the surplus can easily save you from buying $50

of "fresh" herbs in the supermarket over a year—that's a tenfold return on your initial investment!

➤ **Use a manual push mower.** Save yourself lots of green by cutting your lawn with a manual push mower instead of a gas-powered unit. Manual push mowers slice the grass using the energy you provide and cost anywhere from $100 to $150 with virtually zero maintenance costs. On the other hand, gas-powered lawn mowers are expensive. A mid-range gas push mower costs around $500, while a ride-on mower can cost in the thousands. Add the cost of fuel and you're looking at tall costs just to keep your lawn short. As an added free bonus, push mowers are quiet, are non-polluting and give you a great workout.

BOTTOM LINE: Get physical and use a manual push mower to trim your lawn and save hundreds over the gas-powered variety both in purchase price and fuel costs.

➤ **Keep your lawn mower sharp.** You don't need to be the sharpest knife in the drawer to know that dull lawn mower blades do not cut grass well. If you're using a gas or electric mower, dull blades can increase energy use by 10%. Purchase a sharpening stone for $5 to $10 at most hardware stores and sharpen your lawn mower's blades at least every other month. Just be sure to turn off or unplug your mower before sharpening.

BOTTOM LINE: Dull lawn mower blades can give your lawn a ragged look and cost you around $20 in increased energy costs. Sharpen your blades bimonthly with a $5 sharpening stone.

➤ **Mow your own lawn.** Rather than hire a company to mow your lawn, get your motor running and cut it yourself. Lawn-maintenance contractors can charge $100 to $200 each month to care for an average lawn. If you don't have the time, consider hiring your neighbour's teenager to mow for less than the cost of a professional.

BOTTOM LINE: Save up to $800 each year by cutting your own grass.

➤ **Grow a taller lawn.** Growing your lawn to heights between 5 and 8 centimetres (2 and 3 in.) can save you up to 50% of the water consumed by a shorter 2.5 to 5 centimetres (1-to-2-in.) lawn. Keeping grass cut short causes the roots to grow shallow, which exposes them to the drier soil at the surface, so the grass then requires more frequent watering.

BOTTOM LINE: Keep your lawn between 5 and 8 centimetres (2 and 3 in.) to save up to 50% on your watering. A taller lawn also helps to crowd out weeds, saving you additional dollars on weed-busting maintenance costs.

➤ **Never overwater your lawn.** An established lawn requires only 2.5 centimetres (1 in.) of water each week, whereas many people water double that amount. Every centimetre of water on a 100-square-metre lawn (1,075 ft.²) adds up to 1,000 litres, or 1 cubic metre, of water. With many municipalities charging $2 per cubic metre for water, the price of overwatering your lawn can quickly add up. To measure your water usage, buy a plastic watering gauge at your hardware store for about $5. Place the gauge in the lawn and turn off the sprinklers when you have reached the target amount.

BOTTOM LINE: By watering a 100-square-metre lawn 2.5 centimetres each week instead of 5 centimetres, you save $21.67 each month. Decrease the amount of water you feed your lawn and save hundreds each year.

➤ **Water early in the morning.** Watering your lawn and garden early in the morning when it's cool out, and before any winds have picked up, can significantly reduce the amount of water you need to use. By watering in the mornings instead of in the hot afternoons, you can reduce your water use, because heat and evaporation are not diminishing your watering attempts.

BOTTOM LINE: Save up to 40% on your lawn and garden water costs by watering early in the morning.

➤ **Collect rainwater with a rain barrel.** Hook up your home's eavestroughs to a rain barrel and collect free water for irrigating your garden. The roof on an average house can collect over 1,000 litres in a single 10 millimetre downpour, adding up to over $2 in municipal water depending on your location. Rain barrels can be purchased at hardware stores for around $50 each, but large plastic drums can be found for free or at very low cost by browsing the classifieds in your local paper.

BOTTOM LINE: Save up to $50 a year on water costs by connecting your downspout to a rain barrel.

➤ **Use vinegar and dish soap to kill weeds.** Lawn and garden herbicides can eat holes in your pocketbook while being hard on the environment. Skip expensive herbicide chemicals and cultivate your own weed-clobbering solution by mixing vinegar with a bit of food-safe dish soap. Fill an old spray bottle and spray directly onto the leaves of weeds. This frugal and environmentally safe mixture kills most weeds and can be safely used anywhere near pets and children. For tougher weeds, a bit of digging is free and guaranteed to work.

BOTTOM LINE: Use vinegar and elbow grease to kill weeds instead of paying for herbicides, saving you about $15 a year.

➤ **Make your own fertilizer with compost.** Skip spending good dollars on expensive synthetic and petroleum-based fertilizer each year by starting a compost. A properly maintained compost can break down waste from both your kitchen scraps and garden trimmings. The compost from a single household can replace about $20 worth of synthetic fertilizer each year and will help keep chemicals out of your vegetable garden.

BOTTOM LINE: Start a compost in your backyard, under your sink or in your basement and save up to $20 each year on buying fertilizer.

Growing Plants from Cuttings

Propagating a plant from a cutting is an easy and free way to grow more plants for less. And it's so simple: you take a plant piece such as a stem and grow a whole new plant out of it! Bushes, shrubs, perennial flowers and vegetables can all be grown from cuttings, saving you the expense of shopping at your local garden centre. Talk to your friends and neighbours about trading cuttings from one another's plants to increase your variety of specimens.

What You Need
- A source plant
- Pruning shears or a sharp knife
- Rubbing alcohol
- Rooting hormone (a $10 container can be used for about 50 cuttings)
- Soil-less potting mix or a 50/50 mixture of potting soil and sand
- A pot
- A clear plastic bag

Instructions
1. Select a cutting from a source plant—side stems about 5 to 10 centimetres (2 to 4 in.) long are preferable, and younger growths without flowers work best.
2. Sterilize pruning shears or a sharp knife with rubbing alcohol. Remove the cutting from the source plant by cutting or slicing diagonally.
3. Remove leaves from the lower half of the cutting.
4. Dip the cut end of the cutting in rooting hormone, following product directions.
5. Add your potting mix to the pot and poke a hole in the soil deep enough to fit the lower half of the cutting.

6. Insert the cutting into the hole and gently press the soil around it. Water well.
7. Place the pot with the cutting into a partially sealed plastic bag to keep the humidity high. Try to avoid letting the plastic touch the plant.
8. Rooting can take from one week to one month, depending on the plant variety. To check, gently tug on the cutting once a week. If you feel a bit of resistance, rooting has begun.
9. Once the plant has rooted it can be transplanted to regular potting soil.

Success rates vary from 50% to 90% depending on the plants you use, so it's always a good idea to take more cuttings than you need plants. Once the plants have started growing, any extras can be given away as gifts! ■

➤ **Raise backyard chickens.** I cluck you not, there is a growing movement among urban dwellers to spare some space in their backyards to raise chickens for eggs. You won't save huge bucks from raising your own clucks, though. The monthly cost of keeping six chickens is about $30 in standard feed, and this doesn't include the cost of building a small coop and buying the birds. But if you love fresh eggs, expect to fetch about 9 to 10 dozen eggs from half a dozen chickens each month, averaged throughout the year. You can reduce chicken feed costs by giving your kitchen scraps to the birds. Chickens can be fed basically any food, including fruits, vegetables, kitchen leftovers and small amounts of meat. Avoid feeding your fine feathered friends avocado, salty or greasy foods, raw potato peels or potato greens, citrus, chocolate, processed sugars and spoiled food. Raising backyard chickens may not save you huge dollars over buying eggs from the grocery store, but the eggs will be much better quality, and the home-entertainment value alone may be well worth the price. Keeping chickens at home may even prove a fun way to teach your kids about farming, helping them develop a better understanding of where our food comes from. If you have neighbours who love eggs, consider selling your dozens to raise some extra dollars. Just check your municipality's bylaws before building a coop; some may have rules against poultry running free in backyard spaces. Check out backyardchickens.com for resources on building coops, buying birds and how to take care of your feathered friends.

BOTTOM LINE: Keeping chickens for eggs works out to about $3.15 per dozen eggs—about the same price as at the grocery store but for much higher quality eggs.

How to Start a Compost

Composting is a frugal and environmentally friendly way to turn kitchen and garden waste into nutrient-rich fertilizer for your lawn and garden. Virtually all plant material can be composted, ranging from fruit and vegetable peels to coffee grounds. A well-maintained compost will break down smaller pieces of organic matter in weeks, giving you access to fresh soil on a regular basis. Avoid adding dairy-based foods, meat and fish, poop and non-degradable matter like plastic, glass or metals to your compost.

All you need to create your own soil is a compost bin and a shovel. Composting bins can be built for little to no cost using scrap lumber, while plastic compost bins can be purchased at most hardware stores for around $50—many municipalities often sell plastic compost bins for half the price in the spring.

Composting Tips

Here are some ways to get into the habit of composting and methods for building a more effective mixture:

1. Keep a small bucket or container in your kitchen to help collect biodegradable scraps like produce peels and coffee grounds. Every few days, dump your kitchen waste into the compost bin and mix the new material into the existing compost.
2. Try to maintain a compost mixture of about half "browns" and half "greens." Browns are materials high in carbon such as dried grass, leaves, sawdust, straw and paper. Greens are materials high in nitrogen such as kitchen vegetable waste and any fresh plant material such as grass clippings. You don't need an exact mixture, but having a compost of only browns or only greens will not promote decomposition.
3. A working compost should not smell. If your compost has an odour and attracts flies, make sure you have a good mix of browns and greens and always cover fresh material with existing compost.

Maintaining Your Compost

Maintaining your compost takes only a few minutes a month. Here are some tips to keep your compost breaking down effectively:

1. Once a month thoroughly turn and fluff all material in the bin using a shovel or pitchfork. This gets the air circulating around the material, which provides ventilation and promotes decomposition.
2. In the hotter summer months, add a little water every other week to keep the compost moist but not soaking. Moisture feeds the bacteria in the compost and keeps the material composting.
3. After one or two years, depending on how much compost you produce, remove most of the material from the compost bin. You can either let this sit to "finish" in a pile for a month or dig it directly into your flowerbeds and vegetable garden. Don't remove all your compost, though—leave a small amount to help get the next batch going.

BOTTOM LINE: Composting can eliminate the need to use synthetic fertilizer, saving you at least $20 to $50 a year.

Composting also reduces the amount of garbage you produce, which can decrease the cost of garbage pickup and save you from spending additional dollars on plastic garbage bags. Because composted fertilizer absorbs and retains water more readily than regular topsoil, you can also decrease the amount of water you use in your garden. ■

10 Vegetables You Can Grow in a Pot

Don't have space for soil? No worries, you don't need a large yard or the perfect plot to grow your own vegetable garden. All you need is a little imagination, some seeds, soil and a flower pot. I learned about container gardening years ago while living in an apartment building in downtown Ottawa. My neighbours one balcony over always grew a selection of parsley, green beans and heirloom tomatoes in containers and would often share some of their extra bounty. I learned the value of limited gardening space and how much one could grow just by using the right containers and two green thumbs. By growing these 10 vegetables or herbs in a pot, I estimate I saved hundreds a year on groceries—and had lots of fun at the same time. For free, customized advice, make use of the experts at your garden centre—they'll have great local knowledge and will be able to answer your questions about sunlight, location and planting.

What You Need
- **Planter pots.** A 10-inch diameter clay pot costs about $5. Plastic containers cost 50% less.
- **Soil.** Untreated potting soil costs about $2 to $3 per bag, enough for several pots.
- **Watering can.** You can make do with a small bucket, but a spouted can costing $5 to $10 makes watering a lot easier.
- **Seeds or plants.** Growing from seeds is less expensive than potting plants.

Get Planting

Growing food in containers is fun, frugal and easy. The following vegetables and herbs all grow well together, so don't be afraid to mix six or seven herbs together in a single pot, or use cordoned containers to grow different vegetables together.

1. Herbs

Fresh herbs bought from the grocery store are expensive. Starting a small herb garden in a pot can provide you with fresh herbs all summer long. Rosemary, basil, thyme and sage can all be planted together in a single container.

2. Tomatoes

While many garden varieties of tomatoes require a large area to grow, plenty of newer varieties thrive in a pot. Ask at your garden centre for "patio tomatoes" and consider smaller cherry tomato varieties.

3. Salad

Heads of lettuce take up a lot of space, but spring mix varieties grow in less space and can be harvested frequently. Arugula is a frugal favourite for a spicier salad.

4. Snap peas and beans

Run some strings up your balcony and get vertical with peas and beans grown in a pot.

5. Radishes

Radishes are quick and easy to grow and don't take much space.

6. Beets

Beets grow easily in a container. Just be sure to use a large enough pot for the variety you choose.

7. Cabbage

Container cabbage takes a little bit of work. When the cabbage head is first forming on your plant, slice the top part of it into quarters (when looking down) to grow four smaller heads instead of one large one.

8. Garlic

A small rectangular planter can grow enough garlic to last you a long time. It's easy to grow, and if you dry it after harvesting it could last you well into the winter.

9. Hot peppers

If you live in a warmer climate, hot peppers such as jalapeños are simple to grow. They can be used as attractive ornamentals while providing some home-grown heat for your chili.

10. Cucumbers

Don't go for the massive field cucumber varieties, which require too much space. Small pickling varieties grow well in a pot and taste great both fresh and pickled.

Bonus: Catnip

Catnip is easy to grow and can provide hours of entertainment for your feline friends. Catnip can be easily used in homemade cat toys and shared with your neighbourhood cats. ■

PART FOUR

More Ways to Save

We've looked at where you live, how you live there, and every detail of every room, but there are still more ways to save! Check out these final pages for suggestions on how to get out of the house without breaking the bank, how to pamper your pets for less and for handy checklists that will help jumpstart your journey on the road to frugal bliss. Happy saving!

18 Ways to Save on Your Next Family Vacation

1. **Go all-inclusive.** Choosing an all-inclusive resort vacation is the easiest way to stick to your budget, since you won't have to plan for meal expenses and entertainment. (They're also a great choice if you're travelling with teens who have big appetites.) Before you sign up, however, consider whether you'll be paying for services you won't use. If you and your family are not big eaters, or if the upfront price includes alcohol and you don't drink, you may save money by paying as you go.
   BOTTOM LINE: An all-inclusive flight and resort package is about 20% less than the cost of booking separately.

2. **Go in the off-season.** While beach getaways are more welcome during a Canadian winter, many families with kids can travel only when school is out. Late summer can be a good time to visit the Caribbean or Mexico, since trips to these destinations are cheaper and the weather in August isn't that much hotter than in February. If your kids can afford a week off school, travelling in North America in May, June or September allows you to save money and avoid crowds in popular tourist areas, while still enjoying decent weather in most places.
   BOTTOM LINE: Visiting a destination during its low season can often save you 30% to 40%.

3. **Wait till the last minute.** If you're just interested in getting away, some super-cheap last-minute packages are available

online. (In the travel business, "last minute" really means you book a couple of weeks early.) Check out sites such as SellOffVacations.com, TripCentral.ca, Travelocity.ca and Expedia.ca. Last-minute deals are less tempting when it's high season, but you can almost always find week-long getaways for under $700 per person, including flight and hotel.

BOTTOM LINE: Expedia.ca advertises last-minute deals for 30% off.

4. **Shop around for the cheapest flights.** For popular destinations, booking online is usually the best way to find good deals. Start with FlightCentre.ca and CheapFlights.ca, as well as the more comprehensive Expedia.ca and Travelocity.ca. The latter has a service called FareWatcher that tracks up to 10 destinations and sends you email alerts when good deals become available. For overseas flights, consider using a consolidator, a company that buys up unsold seats from airlines and unloads them at deep discounts. Visit BargainTravel.com or AirlineConsolidator. com to get started.

BOTTOM LINE: Comparing flights online should save you at least 10% as opposed to booking directly through the airline.

5. **Find cheap hotels online.** Many budget travellers have discovered Hotwire.com, where you can save big if you're willing to wait until after your booking is confirmed to learn the name of your hotel (you do get to choose the neighbourhood). You can also

find cheap rooms through Hotels.ca and WotIf.com. Here's a tip: after you confirm your booking online, call the hotel and ask for a room on a higher floor. Many hotels put their online bookings on lower (and noisier) floors, but they will usually move you for free if you ask.

BOTTOM LINE: Hotwire.com says it can save you up to 60%.

6. **Look for alternatives to a hotel.** Booking your family an apartment or condo may be cheaper for stays of more than a few days, plus you'll enjoy the experience of getting off the tourist track. House swaps are a bargain if you're willing to let strangers stay at your place: browse HomeForExchange.com, HomeXchangeVacation.com and similar sites. Another option is to rent a time-share property from its owner: look at VRBO.com (that's "vacation rentals by owner") for ideas and reviews of the properties.

   BOTTOM LINE: There are some great deals to be had at VRBO.com, such as suites in Hawaii for $500 (US) a week.

7. **Enjoy meals in your room.** When travelling with kids, meals can be your biggest expense. Choose accommodations with a fridge, stove and microwave, then hit the grocery store and plan for at least one meal a day in your room. Stock up on juice and snacks to avoid the ridiculous prices in vending machines and hotel tuck shops. After a long day of sightseeing you probably won't feel like cooking, so buy bread and cheese

and make your own sandwiches for a super-cheap and quick meal.

BOTTOM LINE: Buying a bag of milk, some fresh fruit and a box of cereal will save you $20 a day on breakfast for a family of four.

8. **Watch for extra charges.** Travel sites love to advertise super-low prices for flights and accommodations, but they only tell part of the story. Taxes and fees can quickly turn your apparent bargain into a ho-hum deal, or even a rip-off. Read the fine print on websites and travel brochures, and if you're booking by telephone, make it clear you want to know the total price before you give out your credit card number.

   BOTTOM LINE: An example from FlightCentre.ca shows that the teaser price can be less than a third of the real cost: they advertised Toronto to Fort Lauderdale for $83—plus $226 in taxes and fees.

9. **Pay with cash.** It's easy to burn through more than you can afford when you're on vacation, especially if you pay for everything with your debit or credit card. You'll spend less if you give yourself a daily limit and only carry as much cash as your budget allows and keep the rest locked in the hotel safe. Give your kids a daily allowance that will cover snacks and any souvenirs they choose to buy.

   BOTTOM LINE: If you're prone to buying impulse souvenirs and overindulging at restaurants, you can cut your daily spending in half by paying with cash.

10. **Fly from a U.S. airport.** If you're travelling to the United States, especially during peak times, it may be far cheaper to depart from a border city: for example, if you live in southern Ontario, flying from Buffalo can be much cheaper than departing from Toronto. Some families save even if they have to book a hotel the night before departure. You might need the help of a travel agent, since Canadian websites may not allow you to buy departure tickets from U.S. cities.
    BOTTOM LINE: During the Christmas rush, a family of four can save several hundred dollars per ticket with a cross-border departure.

11. **Go camping.** Not everyone is the camping type, but it really is the ultimate low-cost family vacation. If you've never camped before, book a cabin at a private campground before you consider pitching a tent. Camping equipment is expensive, and if you're a novice you won't know what to bring, so talk with friends who are veteran campers and see if you can borrow their stuff (or rent a tent from a local camping store) for your first trip.
    BOTTOM LINE: You won't find a cheaper destination than a campsite at a provincial park for $30 a day, including showers.

12. **Get the most out of your credit card.** No one wants to pay more fees to the good people at MasterCard, Visa and American Express. But some of the benefits they offer can be a great deal for travellers. If you have a premium card, chances are your annual fee includes insurance for rental cars (which can be $20

a day otherwise) and even coverage for trip cancellation or baggage loss. Call your credit card company before you book to make sure you understand the conditions.

BOTTOM LINE: BMO's Mosaik MasterCard offers a travel package covering cancellation, flight delays, baggage loss and car rental coverage for just $60 a year. For similar coverage on a $5,000 trip through a travel agent, you may pay five times more.

13. **Forget the lame souvenirs.** Everyone wants to remember great family vacations, but who hasn't experienced buyer's remorse after too many trips to the tourist shops? Preserve your vacation memories by taking lots of photos and making a scrapbook when you get home. If your kids need to bring something back, suggest they pick up shells from the beach or a cool rock from the hiking trail, or save their ticket stubs from museums and other attractions.

    BOTTOM LINE: Say no to one tacky T-shirt and save $25.

14. **Get a good exchange on your loonies.** If you're travelling to the U.S. or overseas, currency exchanges can cost you a bundle. Plan ahead and exchange cash at your home bank rather than at the airport or hotel: counters that cater to tourists offer unfavourable rates. While the Interac system is widely available in the U.S., both the local bank and your home bank usually charge a hefty service fee for withdrawals, and an additional fee (typically about 2% or 3%) for the currency exchange. Ask your bank how you can reduce these charges. For example,

Scotiabank customers can make no-charge withdrawals at Bank of America ATMs and through specific banks in other countries.

BOTTOM LINE: When the official exchange rate is 80 cents on the loonie, $200 American should cost you $240 Canadian. But withdraw that $200 at an ATM south of the border, and you could pay $250 or more because of fees.

15. **Plan ahead and prepay.** Flights and hotels aren't the only places you can save by surfing the web. Take some time to plan ahead and you can save big in other ways: theme parks, museums and attractions will often give discounts if you buy tickets online before you arrive—you'll save lineups, too. Restaurants.com offers coupons for eateries across the United States: you choose the neighbourhood and get a choice of restaurants where you can buy a $10 voucher for $3, or a $25 voucher for $10. To save on airport parking, visit DiscountAirportParking.net, where you can get a heavily discounted price for a small upfront fee.

    BOTTOM LINE: A half-hour online before you leave can knock $100 or more off your trip.

16. **Get a hotel with a pool.** A hotel pool is the best free entertainment you'll find on a family vacation. It will keep kids occupied for hours and allow you to relax with a book and a drink at poolside. Some families even opt for a cheap mini-vacation with young kids simply by booking a pool-equipped hotel near their home for the weekend.

BOTTOM LINE: Put $40 in your pocket by spending one afternoon in the water instead of heading out for a round of mini-golf or go-karting.

17. **Look for freebies.** Many museums have one night a week when admission is free or reduced. Plan ahead and arrange your itinerary so you can take advantage of these freebies. (Be aware that places will usually be more crowded on these days.) Rather than booking a bus tour, explore cities with a self-guided walk—look for route suggestions at the tourist info booth—especially if you have older kids. Stuff a backpack with drinks and snacks so you won't be tempted to stop at every Starbucks.

BOTTOM LINE: Visit the Chicago Children's Museum on Saturday afternoon and a family of four pays $36. Go on Thursday evening instead and get in for free.

18. **Make it a "staycation."** Take a week off to just hang out with your kids: go swimming at the community pool, or take walks or bike rides in the neighbourhood, finishing with a stop for ice cream. If you live in a big city, chances are there are popular tourist spots that you've never bothered to visit: how many Torontonians have never been up the CN Tower? A ride to the top may be pricey ($25 per person), but it's nothing compared to the cost of an "awaycation"—and has the feel of a vacation treat. If your kids are sports fans, take them to watch the local minor-league or junior team to enjoy a fast-paced game

at a fraction of the cost of the big leagues. For ideas—and a genuine vacation atmosphere—pick up a tourist guide to your own city.

BOTTOM LINE: Give up a week at a resort or hotel and save as much as a few thousand dollars.

11 Ways to Save on Your Pets

1. **Adopt, don't buy, a pet.** Rather than spend hundreds or even thousands of dollars on a purebred puppy or kitten, adopt a lovable mutt or adorable tabby from the Society for the Prevention of Cruelty to Animals (SPCA), humane society or municipal animal services. Adoption fees are generally under $200 for dogs and under $100 for cats. Before adoption, many shelters will encourage you to bring the animal home on a trial basis to determine compatibility. Adopting an adult animal instead of a newborn one means that behavioural quirks and health problems are more apparent and can help you better choose the perfect pet for your family. If you're set on a particular breed or need a hypoallergenic dog, check out petfinder.com, where you can search the postings of local rescue societies. Fees will be higher than at the SPCA but still a huge savings over a pet store.

   BOTTOM LINE: Bring home a pet from the SPCA or humane society and save hundreds by not buying from a pet store or breeder.

2. **Get your pet spayed or neutered.** Caring for one pet can be a wonderful experience. Caring for a litter of puppies or kittens and finding homes for them is expensive. With many thousands of unwanted animals put down by shelters each year, it is very responsible to help control the pet population. Spaying and neutering early can also help minimize your vet costs down the road by helping to decrease the odds of infection and illness in older animals.

   BOTTOM LINE: Litters of puppies or kittens may be cute, but they become expensive when you factor in vet bills and the cost of finding homes for them. Spend a little now on spaying or neutering your pet to save down the road.

3. **Brush those teeth.** Like humans, a dog's teeth can decay if not cleaned regularly and can cost you with big vet bills in years to come—so start brushing Fido's teeth. Be very careful and gentle when you start a brushing routine, as it may take a while for your dog to accept dental care. Teeth can also be cleaned to some extent by feeding your dog hard kibble and providing a chew or rope toy. Regular dental care reduces the number of visits your dog will need for teeth cleaning, and also decreases the chance the dog will need expensive veterinary attention for other tooth-related problems later in life.

   BOTTOM LINE: Brushing your dog's teeth can help prevent tartar buildup and tooth decay. Prevent bringing your dog to the vet for a $500 cleaning by spending $5 on brushing Fido's fangs weekly with beef-flavoured doggie toothpaste.

4. **Only vaccinate if necessary.** Common wisdom holds that pets should get their shots every year, but check with your veterinarian to determine what shots are actually necessary for the life your pet leads, and if they need to be applied yearly. For example, some types of rabies vaccination are needed only every three years, and may be completely unnecessary in areas of the country where rabies is non-existent.
   BOTTOM LINE: By limiting vaccinations to the required number, you could save about $50 each year.

5. **Keep medical accessories like Elizabethan collars.** Many dogs and cats come home from surgery with medical devices like a $50 Elizabethan collar to prevent them from licking surgical areas. Pet medical devices can be expensive, and tossing these accessories may prove a costly mistake if your pet ever needs one again or if you have another pet of a similar size later on. You can also use collars to help prevent small scratches from becoming vet-worthy problems through scratching and licking, saving the cost of a vet visit. After use, keep pet medical devices clean by wiping with a light bleach solution.
   BOTTOM LINE: Save at least $50 by not having to replace Elizabethan collars and other pet medical accessories.

6. **Shop around for a veterinarian.** Not all veterinarians charge the same rates, nor do they all provide the same level of service. When looking for a veterinarian, try to meet with at least three in your area. Don't be afraid to ask for regular checkup prices

and for other care costs such as overnight hospital stays. Ask neighbours and friends in your area which vets they use, what they think of the vet and how much the vet charges. Doing your research before your pet needs medical attention is the best way to prevent surprises later when you get the bill.

BOTTOM LINE: Do your research and find a veterinarian you can trust to provide your animal with the utmost care, while not overcharging you. You may save yourself thousands in pet care costs by finding the right vet for your pet and pocketbook.

7. **Groom your pet at home.** With some simple and inexpensive tools you can groom your pet at home, keeping her healthy and well maintained. Bathing your dog in the tub using an unscented no-name baby shampoo saves you $20 on a doggie blow-dry—just put a towel on the bottom of the tub first to avoid scratches. Home haircuts are a great way to save money if you and your pet have the patience to get through them. Regular brushing and nail trimming is easy to do yourself, and helps you keep a close eye on your pet's health.

BOTTOM LINE: For a one-time expense of $30, you can buy a set of combs and scissors that will save you at least $50 every few months if you groom your dog at home. For a deluxe version, pick up a set of clippers starting at about $100—they'll pay for themselves in a few months.

8. **Avoid doggie dress-up or feline fashion.** Your pet doesn't need to look runway ready or have a Halloween costume to be

loved by you. While the odd outfit or protective winter wear is fine, the vast majority of pet fashions are a waste of money. If your pet needs something special, consider going to the dollar store for fabrics like fleece and sew something up yourself.
BOTTOM LINE: The occasional outfit or protective wear is fine, but do watch the high costs associated with buying clothing for cats and dogs.

9. **Protect those paws.** The Canadian winter can be cruel to a pet's tender tootsies. Working dogs that spend hours outdoors may require quality booties ranging from $30 to $50, but dogs that spend more time inside could walk for less by wearing generic balloons on their feet—just cut the tops off. Save some serious cash on paw ointments by purchasing a can of Bag Balm for under $15 at your local pharmacy or feed store and generously applying it between your pet's toes.
BOTTOM LINE: Avoid spending unnecessary money on boots or shoes if your pet is mostly an indoor pet.

10. **Give your pet a toy.** While a few toys are great fun for both pet and owner, animals don't require lots of toy loot to be happy. A dog will be just as thrilled chasing an old tennis ball as with a pile of designer Frisbees. Cats love a nice helping of catnip presented in an old sock and don't mind not having the high-end plush toy.
BOTTOM LINE: Pet toys can be expensive, ranging up to $50, and are marketed to humans, not pets. So be mindful

of toy prices, and consider making your own for less to save money.

11. **Pet insurance probably isn't worth it.** Insuring your cat or dog against accidents or illness is becoming popular. Plans can range from $10 per month for limited accident coverage to $50 per month covering illnesses and accidents. But it's often more cost effective to save the premium money in a high-interest savings account. Over 10 years, paying $40 per month in premiums adds up to $4,800. Compounded over 10 years at 3.5%, this same $40 would come to $5,754.03 in a high-interest savings account. Over a 10-year span, vet bills for things covered by insurance generally total an average of $3,000 to $4,000. Assuming a $100 deductible and 10 claims, this leaves $2,500 to $3,500 actual payout from the insurance. Compared with an investment of $4,800 in premiums, it makes more financial sense to save the money in a high-interest savings account earmarked for pet medical bills.

BOTTOM LINE: Before spending money on pet insurance, run the numbers to see if your pet's insurance premium would be better off invested in a high-interest savings account.

5 Easy, Healthy Family Dinners for $5

What's for dinner? The answer is simple. It's got to be quick, healthy, delicious and affordable. To help you in your quest, I've put together a guide to five family meals for $5.

◇◇◇

1. Simply Elegant Veggie Wrap or Pita Pocket

Get wrapped in whole wheat goodness with these easy-to-make and quick-to-serve wraps or pita pockets. Since kids love bread without crusts, why not get them rolled up with these frugal and healthy sandwiches?

Ingredients
> 1 cup (250 mL) dried beans (mung beans, chickpeas or kidney beans)
> 3 tbsp (45 mL) mustard or Italian salad dressing
> 4 whole wheat wraps or pita pockets
> 1 head lettuce, shredded
> 2 tomatoes, diced
> Salt and pepper

Preparation
- Soak dried beans overnight, rinse well, then cover in cold water and simmer until tender, about an hour. Drain.
- Mix beans with your choice of dressing or mustard.
- On a whole wheat wrap, place beans, lettuce and tomatoes. Add salt and pepper to taste. Roll.

Total Cost: $4.92

Embellish It: Add some cottage cheese or shredded mozzarella.

◇◇

2. Spaghetti with Sneaky Black-Eyed Pea Sauce

Spin into some spaghetti with sneaky black-eyed pea sauce for some frugal family fun. By forgoing ground beef and feasting on beans, you'll get an amazing meal that's packed with protein and kind to your wallet.

Ingredients

> 1 1/2 cups (375 mL) dried black-eyed peas
> 1 lb (500 g) whole wheat spaghetti (buy in bulk)
> 1 tbsp (15 mL) olive oil
> 1 medium onion, diced
> 24 oz (700 mL) tomato-based pasta sauce, preferably spicy
> 2 cups (500 mL) chopped green vegetable of choice—try
>   something in season
> 1 tbsp (15 mL) dried basil

Preparation

- Soak black-eyed peas overnight, rinse well, then cover with water and simmer until tender, about 30 minutes. Drain.
- In a large, heavy saucepan, heat oil over medium heat. Cook onion until tender, about 5 minutes.
- Add pasta sauce, cooked beans, green vegetables and basil. Simmer for 10 minutes, stirring often.
- Meanwhile, cook spaghetti in rapidly boiling salted water until *al dente*. Drain.
- Serve sauce over hot pasta.

Total Cost: $5.21

Embellish It: Find ground beef on sale. Then skip the beans and brown some beef. Also, serve pasta sprinkled with parmesan cheese or mozzarella.

◇◇◇◇◇◇◇◇◇◇◇◇◇◇◇◇◇◇◇◇◇◇◇◇◇

3. Easy Beany Quesadillas

Quesadillas are an easy and quick treat to serve in a snap. Filled with bean-healthful goodness, these wonderful wedges can be split between three family members for a fun meal. If appetites run large in your family, this modest meal can be served with soup, chili or salad on the side.

Ingredients

- 1 1/2 cups (375 mL) dried chickpeas, kidney beans or mixed beans
- 2 tbsp (25 mL) chili powder
- 1 tomato, diced
- 1 cup (250 mL) chopped broccoli
- 4 large whole wheat tortilla wraps
- 2 cups (500 mL) spinach
- 1/4 cup (60 mL) shredded mozzarella
- 1 tbsp (15 mL) olive oil

Preparation

- Soak dried beans overnight, then cover in cold water and simmer until tender, about an hour. Drain.
- In a large bowl toss beans with chili powder, tomato and broccoli.
- On 2 tortillas, spread spinach and then evenly distribute bean filling. Sprinkle mozzarella on top. Cover each quesadilla with a second tortilla.
- Heat oil in a large non-stick skillet over medium heat. Place one quesadilla in skillet and cook for 3 minutes or until bottom is toasted. Flip over and toast the other side for 3 minutes. Repeat with remaining quesadilla.
- Place each quesadilla on a cutting board and cut into wedges.

Total Cost: $5.11

Embellish It: Add more cheese to make wedges even cheesier!

◇◇

4. Hearty Potato, Chickpea and Tomato Stew with Basil

This hearty stew recipe may just surprise you with how quickly and simply you can simmer up a pot of soul-warming family supper in about 30 minutes.

Ingredients
> 1 1/2 cups (375 mL) dried chickpeas
> 1 tbsp (15 mL) olive oil
> 1 medium onion, chopped
> 2 large cloves garlic, minced
> 1/2 tsp (2 mL) paprika
> 1/2 tsp (2 mL) dried basil
> 1/2 tsp (2 mL) dried oregano
> 1 can tomatoes (28 oz/796 mL), undrained and coarsely chopped
> 2 medium potatoes, peeled and diced
> 1 cup (250 mL) water or vegetable stock
> Salt and pepper

Preparation
- Soak dried chickpeas overnight, then cover in cold water and simmer until tender, about an hour. Drain.
- In a large, heavy saucepan, heat oil over medium heat. Cook onion until tender, about 5 minutes.
- Add garlic, paprika, basil, oregano and about 2 of the canned tomatoes. Simmer, stirring often, for 5 minutes.
- Add potatoes and water. Cover and boil for 5 minutes, stirring occasionally.
- Add chickpeas. Reduce heat and simmer for 5 minutes or until potatoes are tender.
- Stir in remaining tomatoes and salt and pepper to taste. Heat for 1 minute and then serve.

Total Cost: $5.14

Embellish It: Sprinkle with fresh parsley and grated cheese.

◇◇

5. Rotini with Veggies and Hummus Sauce

Whole wheat rotini pasta bought in bulk is affordable and tasty. Add some chickpea hummus sauce and serve with colourful veggies to bring this creamy dish to perfection.

Ingredients

> 3 cups (750 mL) whole wheat rotini
> 1 tbsp (15 mL) olive oil
> 1 zucchini, diced
> 2 tomatoes, diced
> 1 tbsp (15 mL) dried basil
> Pinch cayenne pepper
> 2 cups (500 mL) homemade authentic or low-fat hummus (see
>   page 256)
> 1/2 cup (125 mL) water

Preparation

- Cook rotini in rapidly boiling salted water until *al dente*. Drain.
- Meanwhile, heat olive oil in a medium saucepan over low heat. Add zucchini and cook for 1 to 2 minutes.
- Stir in tomatoes, basil and cayenne. Cook for 1 minute.
- Stir in hummus and water. Simmer very gently for 2 minutes.
- Serve hummus sauce over hot pasta.

Total Cost: $5.03

Embellish It: Sprinkle each serving with a dash of parmesan cheese.

Make Your Own Hummus

One of the tricks to making gob-smacking hummus is using fresh ingredients. You can use either canned or dried chickpeas (also called garbanzo beans).

Authentic Hummus

Hummus is great as a dip, in pasta or on sandwiches.

Ingredients
> 1 can (19 oz/540 mL) chickpeas, drained and rinsed OR 6 oz
> (175 g) dried chickpeas, soaked overnight, simmered until
> tender and drained
> 1/4 cup (50 mL) lemon juice
> 1/4 cup (50 mL) olive oil
> 2 tbsp (25 mL) tahini
> 2 cloves garlic, chopped
> 1/2 tsp (2 mL) ground cumin
> 1/4 tsp (1 mL) each salt and pepper
> 3 tbsp (45 mL) water (if desired)

Preparation
- In a food processor, blend chickpeas until smooth.
- Add lemon juice, olive oil, tahini, garlic, cumin, salt and pepper. Process until combined.
- Add a little water to thin, if desired.
- Scrape into a serving bowl. Cover and refrigerate for up to 3 days.

Tip: Tahini is a sesame seed paste (or spread) found in grocery or ethnic specialty stores. Tahini adds a few extra calories to the hummus, but it's the best for an authentic recipe. For a lighter hummus, feel free to omit the tahini.

Low-Fat Vegan Hummus

Want to go low fat? Try this humble hummus recipe.

Ingredients

1 can (19 oz/540 mL) chickpeas, drained and rinsed OR 6 oz (175 g) dried chickpeas, soaked overnight, simmered until tender and drained

2 tbsp (25 mL) lemon juice

1 tbsp (15 mL) olive oil (optional)

2 cloves garlic, chopped

1/2 tsp (2 mL) ground cumin

1/4 tsp (1 mL) each salt and pepper

3 tbsp (45 mL) water (if desired)

Preparation

- In food processor, blend chickpeas, lemon juice, olive oil (if using), garlic, cumin, salt and pepper until smooth.
- Add water to thin, if desired.
- Scrape into a serving bowl. Cover and refrigerate for up to 3 days.

Month-by-Month Maintenance Checklist

Setting aside a little time each month for some tasks around the house can result in huge savings. There's no need to follow this schedule exactly—some jobs can be done at any time of year. If you're feeling energetic one month, go crazy so you're ahead of the game the next.

January

☐ Clean furnace filters.

☐ Check water and drainpipes for leaks.

☐ Make your fridge and freezer as efficient and airtight as possible by inspecting the door seals.

February

☐ Clean furnace filters.

☐ Replace damaged, cracked or frayed electrical cords throughout the house.

March

☐ Clean furnace filters.

☐ Vacuum heating vents and radiators.

☐ Have a fridge and freezer day. Pull the fridge out and vacuum around the coils to keep it running efficiently. Do an inventory and reorganize by date. Use up anything in the freezer that's in danger of being lost to freezer burn. Defrost if necessary.

☐ Have a fire safety day. Replace batteries in all carbon monoxide detectors and smoke alarms. Check pressure in fire extinguishers and schedule a recharge if necessary. Fire departments often recommend that you change your batteries when you change your clocks.

April

☐ Clean furnace filters.

☐ Uncover the AC unit and clear debris from the cooling coils.

☐ Install and inspect your outdoor clothesline. There's no need to run a dryer when it's nice out.

☐ Clean the winter muck off the windows to maximize natural light all summer. You'll feel like you live in a brand-new place.

☐ Sharpen the lawn mower blades for maximum efficiency and minimum gas use. Set the blades higher for taller grass so your lawn won't need as much water.

☐ Start your vegetable garden. It can be hugely rewarding—for your psyche and your pocketbook. Put any seeds you harvested at the end of last summer to good work here.

May

☐ Clean furnace filters.

☐ Examine window screens and replace any damaged ones.

☐ Pull out your summer clothes and put away the winter ones. Make sure the wool is stored safely away from moths! This is a great time to check whether any items need mending.

☐ Set up a composting bin to make your own soil and fertilizer and cut down on kitchen waste. If you're already composting, now's a good time to refresh the bin to keep it efficient: leaving a little behind as a "starter," empty out the bin and spread the soil throughout your garden.

☐ Place rain barrels under downspouts to collect free water for gardening.

June

☐ Clean central air conditioning filters.

☐ Have chimneys professionally swept and inspected.

☐ Check external dryer vent to make sure it's venting efficiently.

☐ Have a fridge/freezer day (see March).

July

☐ Clean AC filters.

☐ If you have a septic tank, get it serviced.

☐ Check water and drainpipes for leaks.

August

☐ Clean AC filters.

☐ Inspect sump pump—best to find out now if it needs to be repaired.

☐ Have heating, ventilation, AC and fireplace professionally inspected. The pros have great tips for savings and are also up-to-date on available government energy rebates.

September

☐ Replace furnace filters.

☐ Inspect windows and external doors on a windy day for drafts. Caulk and replace weatherstripping if needed.

☐ Have a fridge/freezer day (see March).

☐ Check roof for missing or damaged shingles and replace. You can do this yourself, or hire someone if you're not comfy with it.

☐ Harvest what seeds you can now to save on big outlays in the spring for annuals.

October

☐ Clean furnace filters.

☐ Check basement for moisture—fall rains are a good test run to be sure nothing's wrong down there.

☐ Seal electrical outlets on external walls to prevent heat loss.

☐ Pack away your summer clothes (put aside any items that need mending) and pull out the winter stuff. Depending on where you live, you might need to tackle this job sooner.

☐ Get those windows clean again so they'll let in as much heat as possible all winter.

☐ Drain and put away rain barrels. If rain barrels are full and left out all winter, they'll freeze and crack.

November

☐ Clean furnace filters.

☐ Seal and winterize windows with plastic film. Reusable kits are more expensive but can be used year after year.

☐ Check for cracks and crevices in unfinished basements and around exterior of house and use polyurethane foam to seal them.

☐ Once the leaves are down, clean eavestroughs and downspouts so you don't have frozen clumps causing drainage problems in the winter.

☐ Change the batteries in your carbon monoxide and smoke detectors when the clocks change.

December

☐ Clean furnace filters.

☐ Have a fridge/freezer day (see March).

Hardware Store Shopping List

Here's a handy shopping list for all your do-it-yourself projects. Get everything in one trip to save on gas!

☐ Caulking and weatherstripping to seal windows and external doors

☐ Polyurethane foam to fill in cracks and crevices

☐ Insulation for the attic hatch—both batting and rigid foam

☐ Foam gaskets and childproof plugs to seal electrical outlets

☐ Plastic film to seal your windows in winter

☐ Gaskets to fix leaky water pipes

☐ Low-flow showerhead

☐ Dimmer switches for lights

☐ Motion sensor for outdoor light so it's not on all the time

☐ Compact fluorescent light bulbs to replace incandescents

☐ Power strip or surge protector to limit standby power waste

☐ Programmable thermostat

☐ Replacement filters for your furnace and air conditioner

☐ Reusable microfibre cloths to replace costly paper towels

☐ New batteries for your smoke alarms and carbon monoxide detectors

Get Started Now!

Get going on your new, frugal lifestyle immediately with these tips you can put into action today. Success breeds success, so start building good habits right away. Some of these tips don't cost anything at all!

- ☐ Save big by eating dinner at home. Plan leftovers for tomorrow's brown-bag lunch.

- ☐ Eat less meat and more beans.

- ☐ Eliminate some booze—have "dry" nights at a fraction of the cost.

- ☐ Buy a metal mug and make your own "takeout" coffee. Be your own barista!

- ☐ Clip food coupons, and buy bulk and no-name products.

- ☐ Use loyalty program points when shopping and ask for a discount. (You never know! But don't be obnoxious—stores hurt in hard times too.)

- ☐ Dilute lotions, soaps and shampoos with water.

- ☐ Skip the dry cleaner—wash and iron your own clothes. And don't overpour the liquid laundry detergent.

- ☐ Turn down the temperature on your water heater—even one degree saves you big.

- ☐ Skip the dishwasher's drying cycle—open the door and let the dishes air dry.

☐ Maximize washing machine and dishwasher loads to get the most clean for your buck.

☐ Wash clothes in cold water (they last longer that way too) and hang them to dry.

☐ Clean debris away from your AC's coolant coils and move the unit to a north-facing wall to increase efficiency.

☐ Turn the heat down in winter and the AC up in summer—a couple of degrees either way translates into big savings.

☐ Use your drapes to control the indoor temperature—let the sun warm rooms, then trap the heat or keep it out as the case may be.

☐ The only lights that need to be on are those in the room you're in—turn the rest off.

☐ Turn off and unplug unused electrical devices—especially that second fridge, which is usually old and inefficient anyway.

☐ Drive at the speed limit, inflate your tires to their proper pressure and avoid heavy acceleration—you'll be amazed by how much gas you save.

Resources

There are many sources and websites I found helpful in putting together this book. Many of them have even more information and fantastic ideas on how to save money, so take a look.

Part 1: Big Decisions
RENTING

Craigslist
www.craigslist.ca

Kijiji
www.kijiji.ca

HOMEOWNERSHIP

Canada Mortgage and Housing Corporation
www.cmhc.ca

Dinkytown Financial Calculators
www.dinkytown.com

Equifax Canada
www.equifax.ca

Government of Canada Office of Energy Efficiency
oee.nrcan.gc.ca

Industry Canada (Office of Consumer Affairs)
Rent or Buy Calculator
www.ic.gc.ca/eic/site/oca-bc.nsf/eng/ca01821.html

Mike Holmes, *The Holmes Inspection* (Toronto: Collins*Canada*, 2008)

Realtor fees (and other fees)
www.assignmentscanada.ca/buyingincanada.html

TransUnion
www.transunion.ca

FINANCIAL CHOICES

Achieva Financial
www.achieva.mb.ca

Canada Revenue Agency
www.cra-arc.gc.ca

Financial Consumer Agency of Canada
www.fcac-acfc.gc.ca

Financial Webring
www.financialwebring.org

ING Direct
www.ingdirect.ca

MoneySense
www.moneysense.ca

Outlook Financial
www.outlookfinancial.com

President's Choice Financial
www.pcfinancial.ca

RBC Insurance
www.rbcinsurance.com

Social Insurance number application
www.servicecanada.gc.ca

Tax Free Savings Account
www.tfsa.gc.ca

TD Canada Trust Insurance
www.tdcanadatrust.com/tdinsurance

SHOPPING

Aeroplan
www.aeroplan.ca

Airmiles
www.airmiles.ca

Costco
www.costco.ca

Craigslist
www.craigslist.ca

eBay
www.ebay.ca

Freecycle
www.freecycle.org

Futureshop
www.futureshop.ca

Kijiji
www.kijiji.ca

Overstock
www.overstock.com

Real Canadian Superstore
www.superstore.ca

RedFlagDeals.com
www.redflagdeals.com

RetailMeNot.com
www.retailmenot.com

Sears Canada
www.sears.ca

U-Exchange
www.u-exchange.com

Winners
www.winners.ca

Part 2: Home Management
HOME MAINTENANCE

Government of Canada Office of Energy Efficiency
oee.nrcan.gc.ca

ENERGY

ecoACTION
www.ecoaction.gc.ca

ecoENERGY Retrofit Grant Program
oee.nrcan.gc.ca/residential/personal/retrofit-homes/retrofit-qualify-grant.cfm

ENERGY STAR in Canada
oee.nrcan.gc.ca/energystar

Government of Canada Office of Energy Efficiency
oee.nrcan.gc.ca

PowerWISE
www.powerwise.ca

CLEANING

Disastrous Disposables
www.ams.ubc.ca/student_life/resource_groups/sec/rcw-files/disposables.pdf

Part 3: Room by Room
KITCHEN

BAGGU
www.baggubag.com

Federal Trade Commission
"Price Check: A Report on the Accuracy of Checkout Scanners"
www.ftc.gov/reports/scanner1/scanners.shtm

How to soak and cook dried beans
www.squawkfox.com/2008/02/19/how-to-soak-and-cook-dried-beans/

Retail Council of Canada
"Code of Practice: Scanner Price Accuracy Voluntary Code"
www.retailcouncil.org/advocacy/cp/issues/scanner_acc/print/
scanner_accuracy02_eng.asp

LIVING ROOM AND DINING ROOM

Apartment Therapy
www.apartmenttherapy.com

Apartment Therapy
"How to Go 'Shopping' in Your Own Home"
www.apartmenttherapy.com/chicago/how-to/how-to-go-shopping-in-your-own-home-074431

Canada's Office of Consumer Affairs (OCA)
Canada's switch to digital TV
www.ic.gc.ca/eic/site/oca-bc.nsf/eng/h_ca02319.html

Canadian Broadcasting Corporation
www.cbc.ca/video

Canadian Centre for Occupational Health and Safety
"How to Adjust Office Chairs"
www.ccohs.ca/oshanswers/ergonomics/office/chair_adjusting.html

CTV
shows.ctv.ca/video

Google Docs
docs.google.com

Ikea Slipcovers
www.bemz.com

iTunes
www.apple.com/itunes

Live365.com
www.live365.com

Open Office
www.openoffice.org

SHOUTCast Radio
www.shoutcast.com

BEDROOM

Leggett & Platt
www.leggett.com

KIDS' ROOMS AND BEYOND

Camilla Cornell, *How to Pay Less for Just About Anything*
(Pleasantville, NY: Reader's Digest, 2005)

Coolest Birthday Cakes
www.coolest-birthday-cakes.com

Deborah Taylor-Hough, *Frugal Living for Dummies*
(Indianapolis, IN: Wiley, 2003)

Easy Birthday Cakes
www.easy-birthday-cakes.com

La Leche League
www.lllc.ca

Student Price Card
www.spclive.com

BATHROOM

Canada Mortgage and Housing Corporation
"Research Highlights: Dual-flush Toilet Testing"
www.cmhc-schl.gc.ca/publications/en/rh-pr/tech/02–124-e.html

ecoENERGY Retrofit grant program
oee.nrcan.gc.ca/residential/personal/retrofit-homes/retrofit-qualify-grant.cfm

PowerWISE
www.powerwise.ca

LAUNDRY ROOM

ENERGY STAR in Canada
oee.nrcan.gc.ca/energystar

PowerWISE
www.powerwise.ca

GARAGE

Autonet.ca
www.autonet.ca

Canadian Automobile Association
www.caa.ca

Canadian Centre for Occupational Health and Safety
"Telework/Telecommuting"
www.ccohs.ca/oshanswers/hsprograms/telework.html

Carpool.ca
www.carpool.ca

Daily Fuel Economy Tip
www.dailyfueleconomytip.com

Driving.ca
www.driving.ca

Government of Canada
"Tax credit for public transit passes"
www.transitpass.ca

Government of Canada Office of Energy Efficiency
oee.nrcan.gc.ca/transportation/personal

OUTSIDE YOUR HOME

Backyard Chickens
www.backyardchickens.com

Composting Council of Canada
www.compost.org

Part 4: More Ways to Save
FAMILY VACATION

Airline Consolidator
www. airlineconsolidator.com

Bargain Travel
www.bargaintravel.com

Cheapflights
www.cheapflights.ca

Discount Airport Parking
http://discountairportparking.net

Expedia
www.expedia.ca

Flight Centre
www.flightcentre.ca

Home for Exchange
www.homeforexchange.ca

Home Xchange Vacation
www.homexchangevacation.com

Hotels
www.hotels.ca

Hotwire
www.hotwire.com

Selloff Vacations
http://selloffvacations.com

Travelocity
http://travelocity.ca

Trip Central
http://tripcentral.ca

Vacation Rentals by Owner
www.vrbo.com

Wot If
www.wotif.com

PETS

Pet Adoption
http://petfinder.com

ACKNOWLEDGEMENTS

This book grew from the pages of my blog, Squawkfox.com, because of the amazing team at HarperCollins Canada, including Noelle Zitzer, Shaun Oakey, Jeremy Rawlings, Lesley Fraser, Debbie Viets and others who worked so quickly that I did not get to meet them. A very special thank you to my editor, Kate Cassaday, for her enthusiasm, knowledge and ability to know what I wanted to say even before I knew myself. Thank you for finding my blog and for giving me the opportunity to write beyond the blogosphere.

Thank you to my parents, Jan and Ken Taylor, for getting me started young with my own savings account and for teaching me about the power of compound interest.

A huge thank you to Beth Huel and my sister, Allison Taylor, for convincing me that stories about bean-soaking and bean-counting could be fun.

Thanks also to the Russmann family, including Ralph, Max,

Kate and little Alex, for their moral support when I disappeared from the farm to write this book.

Thank you to Doug Lemiski for making the legalese make sense.

Thank you to blogging buddies Hayden Tompkins and Mike for their online friendship and support.

I am eternally grateful to my partner, Carl Russmann, who convinced me to start a blog and share my ideas with others.

Finally, I want to thank the people who read my blog. Some have been reading it since the beginning; others have just found me. Everyone who has emailed or commented on the site has taught me something. I write about frugal living because I love the conversation and creativity of a community of people discovering how to live smarter with less. I hope this book continues the conversation.